Truth in Balance

"Dr. DiCello's new book is an amazing collection. What struck me was his ability to combine some very solid exegetical work (for instance in 1 Peter) with practical insight and good application. Too many scholars are on only one side of the fence—either the work is highly academic with little application or else the application is not really related to the text. Dr. DiCello manages both along with the ability to keep your interest and make you think. I highly recommend it!"
—Steve Gunderson, Educator

"One of my favorite words in the English language is 'balance.' The word evokes cause for pause and thoughtful reflection. I can summarize Dr. DiCello's book in one word: 'Balance.' In the midst of the clash of modernity and postmodernity, Carmen's book provides a thoughtful approach to solid, Christian apologetics that builds bridges among various groups rather than barriers that would divide them. Truth in Balance is a timely blessing for those in Christ and for those who are yet to come to the Savior."
—Ric Walston, Ph.D., President of Columbia Evangelical Seminary

"Truth in Balance does a masterful job covering foundational apologetic territory. However, this book does far more than this. It delves into areas that are rarely addressed, encouraging an apologetic that is lived out in everyday life. I highly recommend this book by Carmen DiCello."
—John Smulo, Founding Director, School of Apologetics, Morling College, Owner, MissionalApologetics.com

"The apostle Peter tells Christians that they must be ready to give an account for the hope that is in them to those who ask (1 Peter 3:15). Truth in Balance opens on the right foundation, setting forth the biblical basis for apologetics and then moves into more practical matters. As DiCello notes, the task of apologetics is not to be left to armchair theologians and pastors; it is an endeavor in which every Christian is called to participate. Truth in Balance is passionately written to encourage all members of the body of Christ to engage in the task of apologetics."
—Jason Crowder, Founder and Director of Know Him Ministries

"Carmen DiCello gives us two books for the price of one: a usable, plausible apologetics for a post-Christian culture, and a hands-on but not high-handed fondling of the contours of truth that is packed with punch and bursting with passion."
—best-selling author Leonard Sweet, Drew University, George Fox University, sermons.com

"Unthinking faith is a curious offering to be made to the creator of the human mind."

John A. Hutchinson

Truth in Balance

Doing Apologetics in a Postmodern Culture

CARMEN C. DiCELLO

WIPF & STOCK · Eugene, Oregon

TRUTH iN BALANCE: DOiNG APOLOGETiCS iN A POSTMODERN CULTURE

Copyright © 2009 Carmen C. DiCello All rights reserved. Except for brief quotations in critical publications or reviews, no part of this book may be reproduced in any manner without prior written permission from the publisher. Write: Permissions, Wipf and Stock, 199 W. 8th Ave., Suite 3, Eugene, OR 97401.

iSBN: 978-1-60608-778-7

Manufactured in the U.S.A.

"Scripture quotations taken from the New American Standard Bible®, Copyright © 1960, 1962, 1963, 1968, 1971, 1972, 1973, 1975, 1977, 1995 by The Lockman Foundation. Used by permission." (www.Lockman.org)

*For those who care to think
and who think in order to care.*

"The truth will make you free" is an old adage with biblical origins. But if liberating truth exists, there must be something about the truth that makes sense, that resonates with the human heart and mind.

Apologetics addresses these issues, seeking to explain, clarify, and demonstrate the beauty and validity of truth so that others may more readily embrace both it and Him who is "the truth" (John 14:6). As such, apologetics plays an integral role in facilitating faith, providing various encouragements to believe, helping to create an atmosphere within which the truth can impact our lives. †

---

†This book addresses issues related to apologetics and faith. Given that these materials originated at diffe ent times and in diffe ent contexts, some overlap between the various sections is inevitable. This will hopefully serve to reinforce the basic ideas that are presented.

Contents

Acknowledgments xiii

chapter 1

Hope's Reason:
The Significance of 1 Peter 3:13-17 for Apologetics 5

chapter 2

Apologetic Perspective:
The Relevance of Presuppositions and Evidence 23

Excursus:
Reflections on Apologetics and Humility 33

chapter 3

Anthropological Underpinnings:
Seeing Humanity As it is 39

chapter 4

The Athenian Challenge:
Communicating the Gospel in Non-Christian Society ... 53

Excursus:
Did Paul Fail and/or Compromise in Athens? 73

chapter 5

Apologetics in a Postmodern Era:
Envisioning an Emergent Faith 79

chapter 6
Truth Tactics:
Miscellaneous Thoughts on pologetics 99

chapter 7
The ltimate Apologetic:
Love and Human Relationships.................................. 117
Excursus:
The L ve Dynamic.. 123

chapter 8
Conclusion 129

appendix A
Conversion and Apologetic Expectations 133

appendix B
Brief Lessons from Jesus on Relating to the World............ 137

appendix C
The Templates Th ough Which We See the World........... 141

appendix D
WFD in a PM World.. 145

Bibliography 149

Acknowledgments

A number of people played a vital role in the completion of this manuscript. Many thanks to Dr. Rick Walston, who proofread a portion of it and offe ed helpful suggestions along the way. Bruno Tassone has always been there to listen and to share helpful thoughts (KP!). Joe Vinanski (a.k.a. Joey V!) has been a terrific conversation partner, as has Mark "Moke" DiCello. My students at Pottsville Area High School are a constant source of inspiration.

Also, i would like to thank Jason Crowder, Steve Gunderson, John Smulo, and Leonard Sweet, along with Dr. Walston mentioned above, for their willingness to endorse this project. Your helpful and very kind words are greatly appreciated.

i am very grateful for the diligent effo ts of those whose help and expertise enabled this manuscript to be brought to print. Kimberly Medgyesy provided the typesetting, and the good people at Wipf & Stock, especially Christian Amondson, worked patiently with me throughout the publication process.

Above all, i want to express my thanks for my fantastic wife, Marilyn, and my terrific kids, Luke and Jake. You guys are an incredible gift from God and the joy of my life. More than anyone else, you fill my soul with hope and provide tangible expressions of God's love in my life.

"To eat bread without hope is still slowly to starve to death."

Pearl S. Buck

"Not only is another world possible, she is on her way. On a quiet day, I can hear her breathing."

Arundhati Roy

When it comes to apologetics, probably no text of Scripture is cited more frequently than 1 Peter 3:15. Too often, however, it is treated as a proof text, quoted merely to support an already existing agenda.

A better perspective will be one that takes seriously the passage and its surrounding context. What does 1 Peter 3 actually say, and how might it contribute to the way we do apologetics?

Chapter One

Hope's Reason

The Significance of 1 Peter 3:13-17 for Apologetics

Introduction

When it comes to apologetics, one of the most important passages in Scripture is 1 Peter 3:15. Here the apologetics mandate is clearly delineated as Peter urges his readers to give an answer for their hope. Indeed, there is little question that this text plays a key role in understanding the subject.

But many, who rightly see in this text a justification for apologetics, are prone to merely quote it in a cursory fashion, while barely noticing (or missing!) some of the guidance this rich passage provides. The efore, this portion of Peter's first letter warrants deeper reflection on its context and contents. The elevant passage reads as follows:

> But sanctify Christ as Lord in your hearts, always being ready to make a defense to everyone who asks you to give an account for the hope that is in you, yet with gentleness and reverence (1 Peter 3:15).

Survey

Peter's first letter to the believers scattered throughout Asia Minor (i.e., modern day Turkey) is filled with instruction on how to live successfully in a fallen world. This he accomplishes by identifying God's people (1:2; 2:9-10), depicting their relationships within society (2:13-20; 3:1ff), and pointing them to the One who alone can produce lasting hope (1:13). The reason why hope is so significant is because of the unavoidable reality of human suffering, including suffering for the sake of Christ (1:6-7; 4:12-19)

Working within the framework of this suffering motif, the apostle encourages his readers to live holy lives (2:15-16; 4:7). Peter expands on this theme in 3:13—4:19. Then, within this broader context, he elucidates principles relevant to the subject of suffering for godly conduct in society (3:13-17). This passage further divides into two sections: (1) an encouragement to live zealous and informed lives (3:13-14a) and (2) the provision of an alternative to the intimidation resulting from persecution (3:14b-17). In essence, Peter enjoins his readers to utilize, and so enjoy the benefits of, a truly Christian apologetic. This will be explo ed in greater detail below.

In verse thirteen of chapter three, Peter asks a rhetorical question: "Who is there to harm you if you prove zealous for what is good?" The clear implication is that godly living (depicted, for example, in 3:1-12) can sometimes insulate the believer from certain troubles. On the other hand, suffering cannot be completely avoided, and when it comes, says Peter, Christians are "blessed" (v. 14). "This blessedness or happiness is the certainty that comes from belonging to God and His kingdom with the promises of future vindication."[1]

The thought continues as Peter draws, with minor alterations, from Isaiah 8:12 (LXX): "And do not fear their intimidation, and do not be troubled" (v. 14b). This type of intimidation can be crushing for the suffering believer, leading to turmoil and trepidation. But there is an alternative to fear, one about which Peter has already written (e.g., 1:6-9, 13-16; 2:18-25). This alternati e is the perseverance that results from a changed perspective. Instead of concentrating on the troubles that inevitably result from a God-honoring lifestyle, Christians are to "sanctify Christ as Lord" (v. 15). To sanctify Christ as Lord is to accept Him as He really is, yielding to His authority and

---

1. Steven B. Cowan, ed., *Five Views of Apologetics*, The Counterpoint Series (Grand Rapids, MI: Zondervan Publishing House, 2000), 273.

will and walking with Him through life's many stages.² The phrase "in your hearts" refers to the believer's inner life. One's commitment begins internally and works its way out in practical ways.

Peter elaborates on the implications of Jesus' Lordship. This entails the implementation of Christian truth and, among other things, a readiness to give an account of one's hope. The passage reads: "always being ready to make a defense to everyone who asks you to give an account for the hope that is within you" (v. 15). "Always" stresses the ongoing need to remain alert, for others are watching (v. 15). This means that hope, normally considered an internal characteristic or mind set, is also observable. In anticipation of Jesus' return,[3][4] hope makes its mark, and even present difficultie become somewhat more manageable. Far from a mere wish, genuine hope so permeates the lives of God's people that even outsiders take notice.

But hope is not only to be perceived but explained. What is needed is a defense or an answer. Though the Greek *apologia* (from which apologetics is derived) is used of a formal defense in a courtroom setting, here it is "being applied to informal exchanges between Christian and non-Christian at any time (*aei*) and under varied circumstances."[4][5] The term "account" (*logon*) similarly implies that "you are to state on what ground you cherish that hope."[5][6] In view, then, is the believer's effo t to communicate spiritual realities, those which undergird and stimulate hope. "This implies a constant

---

2. "The focus of ἁγιάσατε itself is upon the inward acknowledgment of Christ's Lordship." J. Ramsey Michaels, *1 Peter*, Word Biblical Commentary, Vol 49. (Waco, TX: Word Books, 1988), 187.

3. The return of Jesus is an historical event, for it speaks of the ultimate in-breaking of God's kingdom. Some popularizations, however, seem to treat the parousia as some kind of divine fi eworks show, a type of cartoon that is far removed from the real world. While the return of Jesus will, no doubt, be spectacular, it is also anchored to our lives today. Thus, when we speak of the return and of the hope it generates, it is important to see it as the time when things are finally made right, God's ways are magnified, God's Son is honored and appreciated, and those with faith experience in full what they can only partially know now. It is not only an event but an event that initiates salvation in its fullest sense.

4. Michaels, *1 Peter*, 188.

5. Albert Barnes, *Barnes' Notes on the New Testament* (Grand Rapids: Kregel Publishers, 1976), 1421.

willingness to speak up for him, to confess one's allegiance to him, and to witness fearlessly to his saving grace."[6]

Thus far, Peter has urged holy living, even amid suffering, and he has instructed his readers to "give an answer." This answer, this *apologia*, however, is not to be thought of as cold, abstract, and (worse still) condescending. Rather, it entails speaking with "gentleness" (*prautetos*) and "reverence" (*phobou*). Commentators differ on the precise meaning of these terms. Some take both as Godward attitudes, i.e., Christians are to be humble and respectful toward God, and this obviously affects one's relationships with others.[7] Others, however, interpret the first term with reference to man,[8] and the second to God. If this is correct, Peter is saying that "gentleness should be shown toward the antagonists and respect emphatically toward God."[9] It is even feasible that both terms are applicable to the believer's attitude toward those outside the faith. In this case, "gentleness and respect" (NIV) are traits exemplified in one's stance toward others. "'Respect' would mean treating the unbeliever as what he is—a person created in the image of God. It would mean not talking down to him, but listening to him—not belittling him, but taking seriously his questions and ideas."[10] Whatever the specifics, central to Peter's intent is the proper "delivery" of the Christian message. Life, words, and manner of presentation are all integral to the apologist's mission.

As Peter concludes this portion of the letter, he once again reminds his audience that suffering is inevitable. In context, this takes the form of slander (v. 16), which is to be countered by conduct consistent with a "good conscience" (v. 16). When mistreatment is

---

6. Scot McKnight, *1 Peter*, The NIV Application Commentary (Grand Rapids: Zondervan Publishing House, 1996), 213.

7. See Michaels, 189.

8. The use of the term *man* is in no way intended to imply a sexist or chauvinistic attitude. Both men and woman are equal in God's sight and ought to be treated as such. Its use here is simply a convenient way to describe all human beings, male and female alike.

9. I. H. Marshall, *1 Peter*, The IVP New Testament Series (Downers Grove: InterVarsity Press, 1991), 116.

10. John M. Frame, *Apologetics to the Glory of God* (Phillipsburg, NJ: Presbyterian and Reformed Publishing Company, 1994), 30.

met in such a fashion, revilers are "put to shame" (v. 16). "Possibly he is thinking of the way in which persecutors will be ashamed at the Last Judgment when they realize that the people whom they despised are honored by God. More likely he has in mind a change of heart by the persecutors here in this life."[11]

Therefore, if God allows persecution, it ought to be for "doing what is right rather than for doing what is wrong" (v. 17). This way, both those who believe and (potentially, at least) those who don't can benefit. Peter encourages this outlook by appealing once again to Jesus—the believer's Savior, hope, example, and strength (3:8-22).

Having briefly surveyed the wider and narrower contexts of 1 Peter 3:15, we can now highlight some of the key ideas that flow from this passage. What follows are some thoughts, drawn from this relevant New Testament text, that have a bearing on apologetics.

Apologetics Wisdom

There are many passages in Scripture that are relevant to apologetics (e.g., Acts 17:2-3, 15ff; 19:8; Philippians 1:5-7, 16; Jude 3), perhaps none more so than I Peter 3:13-17. This text provides many clues about how apologetics works and how best to approach others with the message of the gospel. To this end, a number of observations can be made.

1. *Genuine hope constitutes a significant attention-grabber.*

   Throughout 1 Peter, hope is a predominant theme. This is the case, of course, because of the difficult circumstances that many a first-century believer endured. The same is true today. Stressful and hurtful times require something of substance to which we can cling. Ultimately, only God can provide such stability for the soul.

   But, the presence of hope is not merely a comfort for believers. It is also has a powerful influence on those outsiders who observe our behavior. This means that true hope is often the instrument by which non-Christians come to see the power and uniqueness of the Christian gospel.

---

11. Marshall, 116.

In a very real sense, then, hope itself—possessed (by the believer), perceived (by the non-Christian), and eventually explained (by the believer)—is the impetus for evangelistic success. When Jesus' followers exude hope, even when surrounded by persecution, this prompts the curiosity of on-lookers. One of the ways we can impact others is by demonstrating a certain steadiness in the face of difficul , a steadiness that is fostered through an awareness of future blessing. Those who know, despite hard times, that good awaits them and will eventually come, exude a type of strength that is a noticeable alternative to secular perspectives. This hope se ves as a powerful attention-grabber.

2. *Hope's explanation is integral to the task of apologetics.*

It is true that hope, all by itself, is able to capture the attention of others. But eventually more must be done and said. While the believer's life is to attract people to the gospel, at some point this gospel must be articulated. In other words, hope demands an explanation. As Goppelt notes: "Here every Christian is summoned to be prepared at all times in relation to every person to give an account about the meaning of being a Christian."[12]

Depending on the circumstances, there are many ways that this might be accomplished. For some a simple declaration of Jesus' suitability as Savior is all that is needed. Others require answers to the objections raised against Christianity. For certain individuals, faulty assumptions need correction.

But whatever the particulars, the believer's witness centers in (and leads to) God's Son. He is the source of genuine hope. Thus, apologetics includes a concerted effo t to declare the truth about Jesus and to show forth the benefits of following Him. The e are countless reasons why a person should trust in the Savior; one of our tasks is to appropriately share these.[13]

---

12. Leonhard Goppelt, *A Commentary on I Peter* (Grand Rapids: William B. Eerdmans Publishing Company, 1993), 244.

13. Here the plural, *reasons*, has been employed, but the text of 1 Peter 3:15 actually reads *reason*. The use of the singular is probably intended by Peter to highlight the supreme cause of a person's hope, i.e., Jesus Christ. But the declaration of this single reason, by the nature of the case, demands fuller

3. *Life and word are inseparably linked in a truly Christian apologetic.*

Apologetics involves both hope and an explanation of the same. Peter seems convinced that these two cannot (or should not) be divorced. A life without a message may impress, but it leaves the onlooker without a solid reason to hope. The goal of our efforts is not merely that others notice our (erratic?) piety but that people embrace the One who can transform lives. On the other hand, a message devoid of godly example remains unconvincing, even hypocritical. Indeed, one wonders how many have spurned Christianity because of the lack of godliness among professing Christians.

But the different facets of apologetics were never intended to be compartmentalized, for hope and message operate in tandem. Christian apologetics requires speech, the communicated truth, even as it demands conduct worthy of this God-given message. Put plainly, apologetics requires a divinely initiated coalescence of life and word.

4. *Evangelistic relevance and apologetic savvy require the diligent use of the mind.*

Peter informs his readers that they are to give an answer or a defense to those who ask. But this is not necessarily an easy task. At one level, of course, the Christian message is simple, and all believers ought to be able to share it with others. At another level, though, the complexity of life and of the situations in which men and women find themselves can make communication quite difficult.

For instance, certain people have been influenced by various bogus philosophies.[14] Others have had bad experiences with so-called church people. Indeed, the objections of many are

---

explanation. The Christian's reason for hope is Jesus, which is demonstrated through the use of many arguments or reasons.

14. For an exposé of some popular belief systems, see Ravi Zacharias, *Deliver Us From Evil: Restoring the Soul in a Disintegrating Culture* (Nashville, TN.: Word Publishing, 1997). Also, a good examination of worldviews can be found in James W. Sire, *The Universe Next Door: A Basic World View Catalog* (Downers Grove: InterVarsity Press, 1988).

grounded in the bad impressions they have received from genuine believers.

It is important for us to think through the ways in which we communicate with those we encounter. This does not mean we should feel excess pressure to do the impossible, that is, to answer literally all queries.[15] But it does mean that we have to take the time and expend the energy necessary to get to know people and their circumstances. Then, we must provide serious and apropos responses to (sometimes reasonable, sometimes unreasonable) questions, and this requires some measure of dialogue-driven thought. Indeed, apologetics "rests on two premises: (1) that you know something about your friends, and (2) that you know something about Christianity."[16]

The bottom line is that there is much more to apologetics and evangelism (and to this passage) than the monotonous repetition of a canned message or the robotic statement of simplistic formulas. Human beings and their circumstances are too complex to demand a "one size fits all" approach to the gospel. While there is indeed one God and one Savior, the manner in which we share the gospel is not always so neat and tidy.[17]

We need not become scholars in order to share the good news, but it is certainly important to recognize that clear thinking was never intended to be an activity reserved for professional theologians or vocational ministers.

---

15. It is worth noting that the specific answer to which Peter refers here concerns hope, not some philosophical dispute.

16. Michael Green and Alister McGrath, *How Shall We Reach Them? The Christian Faith to Nonbelievers* (Nashville, TN.: Thomas Nelson Publishers, 1995), 50.

17. This is not to suggest that it is wrong to memorize and rehearse what you want to convey to others. The point, rather, is that it is incumbent upon believers to acquire as much knowledge as they reasonably can. Though the essentials of the gospel can be grasped and communicated by a child, the Christian message should not be reduced to the simple repetition of the same words. For example, compare and contrast the evangelistic method of Acts 7 with that of Acts 17. Note also Peter's own instruction to "grow in the grace and knowledge of our Lord and Savior Jesus Christ" (2 Peter 3:18).

5. *One aspect of a Christian theodicy*[18] *is the hope of Jesus' return, coupled with a life transformed by this hope.*

Suffering is surely one of the great equalizers of human existence and one of the major objections to theism in general and Christianity in particular. Indeed, in one sense, we all share the same lot. Though perhaps for different reasons, all of us eventually experience the pangs of heartache. No one can avoid contact with what theologians and philosophers refer to as the problem of evil.

Though the Bible has much to say (directly or by way of implication) about this subject (e.g., Job 38-42), Peter's theodicy in this text is straightforward. He urges believers to live soberly within this unpredictable world (1:13-16; 2:1-2; 4:7ff) with a view to the time when evil's conqueror, Jesus Christ, returns.

Between now and then much suffering may come into a person's life, some of which is baffling and nearly unbearably painful. In such a world, frustration, depression, and confusion are common, as is the desire to escape. But, without denying these emotions, Peter charts a better way, a way of hope.

When Christians react in ways that defy the norm, when they exude hope, others—who have themselves experienced pain—take notice. Hope, in other words, grabs their attention. This does not mean that believers never fall apart. Far from it! Nor does it imply some type of stoic resignation, treating faith as a kind of spiritual painkiller. It's just that the believer's overall perspective, which often flies in the face of conventional wisdom, includes a sense that everything will eventually work out for good. This attitude—though declared by some to be naive—is actually a powerful argument against the ultimate triumph of evil.

Though we are nowhere given a full explanation concerning the problem of evil, we are given hope that one day the trials will end. As Jesus Himself encountered and defeated evil at the cross

---

18. A theodicy is an attempt to explain the presence of evil in a good and sovereign God's world. One component of a full-orbed apologetic, therefore, is to provide a solid, biblical perspective on such matters.

(e.g., 1:11, 18-21; 2:21-24), so all evil will eventually be put down. Therefore, amid the pain, Christians can hold up a genuine and powerful antidote to the problem of evil, the hope given to those who follow Jesus. Whatever nagging questions remain (and they do!), in Him there is enablement to persevere now and the expectation—though often through tears—that one day evil will be put down forever. Where there is hope, hope's fulfillmen comes into focus. When hope shines, in other words, Jesus is made known, and He is able to lead us home.

6. *Hard circumstances, especially those resulting from persecution for Jesus' sake, often provide an opportunity for apologetics to flourish.*

As Peter's overall context shows, and as noted above, the believer's response to suffering is a strong argument for the truthfulness of the Christian gospel. In fact so surprising is this response that those who lack such hope are compelled to ask questions.

But all of this points to another factor that is sometimes neglected by those immersed in life's trials. Hurtful circumstances often provide the context within which apologetics flourish. Though all people experience suffering, the follower of Jesus is provided additional resources for handling it. This allows others to witness, first-hand, the power of the good news. Since this is so, Christians must remain alert to apologetic opportunities when trials come.

7. *The proclamation of Jesus' Lordship and the use of reasoned arguments work hand in hand in the doing of apologetics.*

Within the realm of apologetics, two broad camps typically emerge, presuppositionalism and evidentialism.[19] Often, these are treated as separate and irreconcilable positions. Here, however, they are intertwined. Without getting into a detailed discussion, it appears that Lordship, the presuppositionalist's battle cry, and reasoning, the evidentialist's mainstay, exist side by side. On the

---

19. Presuppositionalism and evidentialism are broad categories, admitting a wide range of perspectives. For an effo t to combine the strengths of each, see Ronald B. Mayers, *Balanced Apologetics* (Grand Rapids: Kregel Publications, 1984). See also D. A. Carson's discussion in *The Gagging of God: Christianity Confronts Pluralism* (Grand Rapids: Zondervan Publishing House, 1996), 184-188.

one hand, Jesus' Lordship is to be upheld and proclaimed; He is Lord, and we are accountable to Him. On the other hand, coherent answers are to be provided for those who are interested; a sensible response to questions and objections must be provided. A balanced apologetic can do nothing less.

8. *The gospel is integral to apologetics.*

Certain apologists are so concerned with winning arguments that they forget the purpose for which they are called, the winning of hearts and lives to God. This being the case, it is instructive to observe Peter's Christocentric focus. Though there is much to share with others, hope is of paramount importance. This hope centers in a person, Jesus. Apologetics remains true to the gospel only to the degree that it points people to the unique Savior. In Jesus, apologetics finds its sure basis and goal.

9. *At some level, we are all apologists.*

It is too often the case that believers find themselves spectators, mere observers, of Christian ministry.[20] From this mistaken perspective, apologetics seems foreign to some, being the responsibility of someone else, perhaps a person trained in the field. But Peter doesn't treat apologetics this way. Instead, he encourages all believers to join the apologetics venture. While this does not mean that every believer is equally gifted (or even interested) in these matters, at some level all are urged to consider their roles within the spheres in which they live.

Christians are instructed to think properly (Philippians 4:8; Colossians 3:1-4); when this outlook evokes a response, it is important to be prepared.[21] Answers must be provided, reasons given, hope explained. It is the privilege and duty of all Jesus' followers to join in these noble effo ts.

---

20. Contrast this with Ephesians 4:11-13, where "the saints" (i.e., all believers) are the ones performing Christian ministry.

21. An old saying goes, "You are too heavenly minded to be of any earthy good." Quite the contrary, Scripture tells us that the right kind of "heavenly mindedness" (combined with a proper "earth groundedness") equips believers to accomplish much good!

10. *Apologetics is integral, not incidental, to evangelism.*
Apologetics is often treated as ancillary to the task of reaching the world for Christ. Sometimes this mistaken notion is caused by overly zealous defenders of the faith, who promote an imbalanced (or even unbiblical) philosophy of apologetics.

A more balanced approach reveals the true relevance of apologetics. Though there are many facets to this discipline, at its core apologetics must be seen as integral to the promulgation of the gospel. Indeed, to excise the *apologia* to which Peter refers is to strip the gospel of its explanatory force, thus robbing others of the opportunity to know precisely what it is that stirs the hearts of Jesus' followers.

If evangelism is, strictly speaking, the sharing of the how-to's of the Christian gospel, apologetics is the platform on which evangelism is built. Evangelism says, "Come to the Savior." Apologetics exclaims, "Here is why." Whatever else is true, apologetics must not be minimized or treated as secondary. Instead, it must be viewed as an indispensable component of the mission to show forth the beauty of Jesus, the believer's hope.

Concluding Reflections

There is no shortage of approaches, programs, and suggestions for reaching others with the gospel. Some of these are philosophical and others pragmatic. Some are geared to an academic audience, while others are intended for the average person on the street. But whatever the strategy, Peter's instruction here is invaluable.

One of the keys to this passage is that its instruction is grounded in real-life experiences. A topsy-turvy world, a world that is filled with suffering and uncertainty, requires a stabilizing message. It requires hope.

As followers of Jesus, one of our chief tasks is to be channels of hope, that is, means by which others look outside of themselves to the Source of hope. When we express this kind of realistic but genuine optimism, it catches people's attention. Hope, in other words, is so powerful that it can seep into the hearts of the hurting, causing them to wonder what makes the hopeful individual "tick." It is at this point that believers find legitimate, unforced opportunities to talk about the hope Jesus provides.

Of course the measure of our impact is dependent on our allegiance to the Lord. In other words a Christian *apologia* begins with a heart commitment; Jesus is "sanctified as Lord." This works its way out in the way we live and the words we speak.[22]

In the final analysis, it is essential that we learn to appreciate the grace that causes us to be members of "a chosen race, a royal priesthood, a holy nation, a people for God's own possession." Prolonged contemplation of these immense blessings can only compel us to "proclaim the excellencies of Him who has called us out of darkness into His marvelous light" (1 Peter 2:9). This appreciative declaration of the gracious Savior is pivotal to apologetics. As the Lord reigns in our hearts, shining forth in our lives, he provides opportunities to share the reason for the hope that is in us.

---

22. "Our apologetics must be pervaded by a sense of Christ's lordship, and this demands diligent preparation so that we may be able to obey our Lord's great commission, being prepared to answer inquirers–not only with proclamation, but with answers and reasons." John M. Frame, *The Doctrine of the Knowledge of God*, (Phillipsburg, NJ: Presbyterian and Reformed Publishing Company, 1987), 358.

"We reason deeply when we forcibly feel."

Mary Wollstonecraft

*"Our presuppositions shape our perspective,
our perspective shapes our priorities,
and our priorities shape our practice."*

Kenneth Boa

There is much disagreement about the best way to approach the discipline of apologetics. This has resulted, broadly speaking, in two basic perspectives, presuppositionalism and evidentialism.

Many who appropriate these labels have provided a vigorous and helpful defense of their respective models. There are times, however, when proponents of either position talk past one another, missing the potential benefits of the other viewpoint.

But is it possible to combine approaches? Can presuppositions and evidence be joined together in a coherent and helpful way?

Chapter Two

Apologetic Perspective

The Relevance of Presuppositions and Evidence

Introduction

Apologetics involves demonstrating the truth and attractiveness of a Christian worldview. But not all apologists agree on the manner in which this is most effectively accomplished. This has led to various schools of thought or perspectives, often philosophical in nature, as to the best and most helpful way to promote the gospel.

Among apologetic methods two broad categories emerge, presuppositionalism and evidentialism.

> A presupposition is a belief that takes precedence over another and therefore serves as a criterion for another. An ultimate presupposition is a belief over which no other takes precedence. For a Christian, the content of Scripture must serve as his ultimate presupposition.[1]

Presuppositionalism, then, is the apologetic method which highlights, reflects, and declares the believer's assumptions, those grounded in and flowing out of a biblical worldview.[2]

---

1. Frame, *The Doctrine of the Knowledge of God*, 45.
2. Some, perhaps overly influenced by philosophical usage, have equated presuppositionalism with *a priori* knowledge, knowledge possessed temporally

Evidence, on the other hand, is that which gives credence and support for a certain contention. Moreover, if genuinely reflective of Scripture's overall perspective, it is that which prompts acceptance of and so an allegiance to the true God. This evidence, accurately portrayed, is not only right but persuasive and attractive to the Spirit-illumined mind (1 Corinthians 2:9-13). At any rate, evidentialism stresses the need to provide support or evidence for the Christian faith.

Of course it would be a misnomer to assert that presuppositionalists and evidentialists operate in completely separate spheres. Often each crosses over into the territory of the other– presuppositionalists by their utilization of evidence and evidentialists in their adherence to a distinctly Christian framework. Extreme versions aside, neither method can be viewed in a completely isolated manner.

But this is not to say that those from either school are in total agreement when it comes to apologetic procedures. Indeed, the two are often viewed as distinct and basically different ways to approach apologetics. The contention here, however, is that this need not be the case. As mentioned above, each of these systems cannot help but borrow from the other. Contrary to popular portrayal and the dogmatic assumptions of some on either side, presuppositions and evidence can and should be viewed as complementary.

In order to show this, it is important to back up and gain a larger biblical-theological perspective on these matters, which necessitates an inquiry into the very nature of humanity itself and how human beings acquire knowledge. This requires that we briefly consider the subjects of epistemology and ontology.

---

prior to and independent of any experience. While there is much debate about the relationship between *a priori* and *a posteriori* knowledge (i.e., that which is gained through experience), this need not overly hinder one's understanding of presuppositions. As used here presuppositions are merely the bottom-line commitments (consciously maintained or not) all people hold. For a discussion of these matters, see John M. Frame, *Cornelius Van Til: An Analysis of His Thought* (Phillipsburg, NJ: Presbyterian and Reformed Publishing Company, 1995), 131-139.

Epistemological and Ontological Reflections

Epistemology and ontology are two separate but closely related subjects. Epistemology is the study of knowledge and how one comes to acquire it. Feinberg describes it as "an inquiry into the nature and source of knowledge, the bounds of knowledge, and the justification of claims to knowledge."[3] Ontology, on the other hand, concerns the nature of being, the "theory of the nature of things."[4] As such it involves the metaphysics of being human and both the capacities and limitations inherent among created beings.

In basic terms epistemology concerns *how* humans are, their outlook and perspective, the way they look at and interpret life. Ontology deals more with *what* humans are, the metaphysical components that make one human in the first place

As might be expected, there is a wide range of opinion as to the precise interpretation of such matters, and no one has exhausted every nuance of these terms. The e is, however, much to be gleaned from a basic understanding of them. In fact both epistemology and ontology have a role to play in laying the groundwork for a Christian apologetic.

From the standpoint of epistemology, believers and unbelievers differ considerably in their respective explanations of reality. Indeed, as some have argued, Christian and non-Christian viewpoints are often antithetical. Believers, to the extent that they accurately and honestly embrace God's mind in Scripture, interpret life from that perspective (Psalm 1:1-3). Non-Christians, on the other hand, typically reject any genuine biblical authority (Psalm 1:4-6; Romans 3:9-11). This is why Paul so strongly asserts that "the natural man does not accept the things of the Spirit of God; for they are foolishness to him, and he cannot understand them, because they are spiritually appraised" (1 Corinthians 2:14). This does not mean that non-Christians are always consistent with their own worldview; the opposite is often true. Fundamentally, though, they explain life in terms contrary to the revealed will of God in Scripture, living by a diffe ent set of epistemological rules than believers.

---

3. Paul D. Feinberg, "Epistemology" in *Evangelical Dictionary of Theology*, Ed. Walter A. Elwell (Grand Rapids: Baker Book House, 1984), 359.

4. Frame, *The Doctrine of the Knowledge of God*, 401.

Next there is the matter of ontology. All humans are made in God's image. "To be made in the 'image of God' means that man has an essential likeness and/or similarity in a finite, relative manner to the infinite, self-existing God."[5] As such, there are certain universal characteristics among all people, including intellect, morality, creativity, and other factors. These capacities are reflective of man's being constructed to be, in some limited sense, like God, and they enable man to recognize, both internally and in the external world, that there is a God. However precisely this image is defined, all humans share in it and so possess the same ontological capacity. Mayers notes: "Because believer and unbeliever alike live in God's universe and are made in His image, the ultimate structure of being is identical."[6]

All of this implies that man is a strange mixture of knowledge and ignorance, a conglomeration of truth and error. At one level, human beings know God, while at another level they deny Him. These matters are dealt with in Romans 1-3 where Paul says that humanity's knowledge of God extends even to an apprehension of the Creator's attributes (Romans 1:20). At the same time, man's moral corruption will not allow him to interpret the truth rightly. Thus, his tendency is to "suppress the truth in unrighteousness" (Romans 1:18). In the words of Pascal:

> What a chimera is man! What a novelty! What a monster, what a chaos, what a contradiction, what a prodigy! Judge of all things, imbecile worm of the earth; depository of truth, a sink of uncertainty and error; the pride and refuse of the universe![7]

The fact that all people are ontologically alike—that is, furnished with the same interpretive "equipment"–enables communication between believer and unbeliever to take place. Humanity's innate knowledge of God serves as the point of contact from which interaction with the non-Christian may occur. Christian apologetics appeals to this inherent

---

5. Mayers, *Balanced Apologetics*, 27.

6. Ibid., 215. Mayers himself categorizes this likeness among all people as related to three factors: creation, the image of God in man, and historical revelation.

7. Blaise Pascal, *Pensées* (New York: E. P. Dutton & Co., Inc., 1958), 121.

God-awareness, suppressed as it may be, looking through the layers of false ideas and invalid assumptions, seeking to reach the heart of man. Of course only God can actually plumb the depths of the human soul and overcome the aversion to the things of God (Ephesians 2:1-10).

These epistemological and ontological considerations are pivotal in developing a proper approach to communication. Because fallen men are epistemologically fla ed, effo ts to reach them must not assume non-Christian presuppositions, for these will often conflict wit God's revealed will; indeed they tend to reflect a spiritual opposition to the things of God. But hope is not lost, for the truth is (potentially) perspicuous to non-Christians. That is, man's metaphysical makeup still reflects a capacity to recognize God. Though fallen human beings require divine aid, they still retain an affinity for higher thing

In sum, apologists must recognize both epistemological and ontological factors. In blending these two categories, a more comprehensive apologetic approach is possible.

A Balanced Approach

The above discussion is intended to show that presuppositions and evidence should not be viewed as separate and irreconcilable notions. "Presuppositionalists want to begin with God, evidentialists with ourselves; the balanced apologist says start with both God and ourselves simultaneously, as these cannot be broken apart."[8] As a result, any valid evidentialist method assumes and promotes Christian presuppositions. Similarly, a presuppositional method is truly biblical only if it argues, from a Christian worldview, the evidence of the Christian faith.

This combined perspective is supported by the biblical data. John 14:17, for instance, clearly identifies the presuppositional deficiencies of the unbeliever. "The world cannot receive [the Spirit of truth]." Yet this same gospel urges the reader to appropriate the evidence, particularly that of Jesus' signs, and to follow that evidence to God's Son, Jesus the Christ (John 20:30-31). Indeed, a number of texts state or imply both of these factors simultaneously (e.g., Acts 2:14-40; 7:1-53; 9:20-25; 14:8-19; 1 Peter 3:13-17).

What this does for apologetics is provide a balanced outlook for reaching others with the good news. To ignore presuppositions leads

---

8. Mayers, 198.

either to an underestimation of mankind's fallen condition or a compromise of Jesus' Lordship. Likewise, evidential ignorance results in a type of fideis [9] in which communication is treated as extremely difficult, if not impossibl

The wisest apologetic method is one in which presuppositions and evidence are integrated.[10] The believer enters an apologetic encounter already presupposing the truth of Christianity and recognizing that those outside of the faith often hold anti-Christian biases. Furthermore, the believer's commitment to Christian presuppositions reinforces his confidence in the Bible's truth claims, even as it stimulates evangelistic zeal.

But the recipients of the good news must still see for themselves the many treasures of Christian truth, the believability of Scriptural claims, and the attractiveness of the gospel and of the living God. The efore, apologists share the truth on the basis of biblical presuppositions. Arguments and presuppositions work hand in hand in the outworking of a cogent, biblically directed apologetic.

Guiding Principles

From what precedes a number of relevant principles appear, which we can summarize.

1. *Believers must presuppose a Christian worldview in their apologetic efforts. In simple terms this is an outworking of the fact that Jesus is Lord.*

The e are a number of ways in which Christian presuppositions play a role in the believer's effo ts to reach those outside of the faith. For one, the matter of presuppositions serves as

---

9. "The view that the objects of religious belief and commitment must be accepted by faith rather than proved by reason." Millard J. Erickson, *Concise Dictionary of Christian Theology* (Grand Rapids: Baker Book House, 1986), 57. Extreme versions of fideism are unquestionably contrary to a wealth of biblical data. For a brief survey of some fideistic positions, see Paul Helm, "Faith, Evidence, and the Scriptures" in *Scripture and Truth*, Eds. D. A. Carson and John D. Woodbridge (Grand Rapids: Baker Books, 1992), 303-320.

10. For an excellent example of this perspective, see Kenneth Boa and Robert M. Bowman Jr., *Faith Has Its Reasons: An Integrative Approach to Defending Christianity* (Colorado Springs, CO: Navpress Publishing Group, 2001).

a powerful reminder of one's basic commitments. Life in the real world can involve numerous situations, opportunities, and difficulties In encountering others, believers face a myriad of personalities, questions, objections, and needs. The sheer complexity of communication makes it easy to lose track of what really matters. This being the case, it is imperative that we allow Scriptural counsel to pervade our witnessing opportunities. God's Word, i.e., biblical presuppositions, becomes the guiding force in any attempt to spread the gospel (Psalm 119:11-13; 41-48; 129-130).

Of course there is good reason why believers must be on their guard in speaking with others. This reason, which is integral to the Bible's teaching concerning mankind, is human impropriety (Psalm 51:5; 58:3). The world simply does not operate by the same standards as believers. Presuppositionalism reminds us that those whom we meet often share a diffe ent worldview. This, in turn, produces a determination to avoid compromise, as well as a realization that only God can ultimately overcome human antagonism and invalid presuppositions.

An awareness of presuppositions forces believers to live by faith, a reasonable faith to be sure, but faith nonetheless. Both believer and unbeliever maintain (consciously or not) basic personal and intellectual commitments, with Christians (humbly!) maintaining that a (truly) biblical worldview is not only sensible but a gift from God.[11]

In the final analysis, the determination to uphold and promote Christian presuppositions is an acknowledgment of the Lordship of Christ (1 Peter 3:15). It is within the sphere of clearly enunciated beliefs that men and women can receive spiritual life (James 1:18).

2. *It is important for apologists to recognize that all people are made in the divine image and thus furnished with a certain innate knowledge of God. This serves as the believer's point of contact with the world.*

Men and women intuitively know God. To be sure, human rebellion has blocked the way, and we often run from the

---

11. See John M. Frame's discussion in *Apologetics to the Glory of God*, 9-14.

truth. Still, this does eliminate the possibility of communication between believer and unbeliever. Indeed, the only reason why evangelism and apologetics are feasible in the first place is because the image of God in man is a genuine point of contact. As mentioned above, all humans are metaphysically alike; that is, they posses the same human tools by which the truth can be potentially accessed. Though the gospel is naturally suppressed (Romans 1:18), God is able to overcome antipathy and apathy and so enable otherwise bewildered men and women to grasp His message. In the providence and purposes of the living Lord, unbelievers can come to faith.

3. *The Bible's story line and contents must be persuasively declared, demonstrated, and applied.*

A proper apologetic stance begins with a commitment to Jesus' Lordship as manifested in His Word. This provides the believer with the discernment needed to avoid faulty thinking and to uphold the truth.

But a biblically grounded approach must still meet people where they are. This necessitates an awareness of the human condition and a determination to share the truth with others.

The manner in which this works its way out can range from sophisticated encounters to simple discussions. But whatever the precise argumentation, answers must indeed be provided. While spiritual life requires divine initiative, God normally operates through human interaction and the contemplation of God-given ideas. As Peter notes, Christians must "be ready to give a defense" (1 Peter 3:15).

Conclusion

A full-orbed apologetic program incorporates both presuppositions and evidence. Rather than viewing these as separate and distinct categories, thoughtful believers take advantage of the strengths of each. Therefore, the truth must be believed and faithfully maintained. Apart from a sound worldview, confusion runs rampant.

Simultaneously, the many beauties of the gospel message need to be displayed for all to see.

Put plainly, biblically minded apologetics seeks to reach the whole person with the whole gospel (Acts 5:20). Spiritual duty demands such an approach, one in which the divine image in man is properly and respectfully understood and divine Lordship rightly maintained.

With a sense of sincere gratefulness, believers are to humbly, authentically, and lovingly shine forth the truth wherever they go, sharing the message of Jesus with those they encounter. Only then will we be able to say that we have given an answer to those who ask.

Excursus:
Reflections on Apologetics and Humility

In arguing for a *Christian* apologetic that is governed by *Christian* presuppositions, one of the more obvious roadblocks we face is the simple reality that we might be wrong. In our determination to be true to the gospel, there is always, given our humanity and accompanying imperfections, the possibility of error. What if we are inaccurate about this or that assessment? What if we overly emphasize one truth to such an extent that other truths are minimized or ignored? What if what we presuppose is in fact fallacious?

These and similar possibilities require that we approach apologetics in a truly humble manner. Though boldness can be an admirable trait, and while confidence is not to be despised, any truly Christian endeavor must be saturated with humility. To this end a number of factors come into play.

First, as Christians we are called to grow, which implies growth in every area, including apologetics. If even the perfect Jesus grew in wisdom and knowledge (Luke 2:52), how much more so must we? Second, it is important to remember that believers are called to follow Jesus. This implies that we don't have all of the answers but rather follow the One who does. Thi d, humility is probably best facilitated through what might be termed "big picture" apologetics. We are on much more solid ground when we defend, exclaim, and show forth those aspects of the faith that have been affirme down through the ages and which are not extraneous to the larger cause of the gospel. Fourth, all apologists are recipients of grace. As such, we ought to sympathize with the hurts and doubts of others, for we share a common lot and a common human condition. To approach apologetics in a distant and combative manner is not only unhelpful to the apologetics enterprise but is a sure sign that we lack empathy and authenticity.

Humility and gentleness are woven into the fabric of any Jesus-oriented endeavor. Thus, the presentation of evidence and the promulgation of presuppositions are connected to realism, compassion, and love. If we are humble and gentle, if we honestly seek to follow the way of Jesus, there will remain within us a cognizance that we have blind spots, an awareness that we are ever prone to make mistakes, in this case, mistakes in our approach to apologetics.

While we should never shy away from sharing the truth with confidence, our *apologia* should always be tempered with humility and a sense that we, too, are fellow travelers on the way, dependent on the mercy of God, and always excitedly anticipating whatever new light He might shine on our paths.

"The ultimate mystery is one's own self."

Sammy Davis, Jr.

"Man is a living oxymoron: wretched greatness, great wretchedness, rational animal, mortal spirit, thinking reed."

Peter Kreeft

Our relationships with others are greatly affected by what we assume about them.

Some pundits, drawing attention to the more ignoble characteristics of people, highlight humanity's worst features.

Other observers are just as apt to point out the noble aspects of the human condition.

But both these categories deserve our attention, and we will not understand men and women correctly unless we learn to balance the dignity and depravity of humankind.

Chapter Three

Anthropological[1] Underpinnings

Seeing Humanity As It Is

Introduction

Imagine this scene: A mean, self-centered man named Joe frantically waves a gun at those who would dare stand in his way, commanding a teller to hand over the bank's currency, hurling expletives at the stunned bystanders who desperately attempt to avoid his fury. As the man leaves the scene of the crime, he hurriedly escapes in his car in order to evade the authorities, his tires screeching as he turns one corner, then the next. Suddenly, the man slams on his breaks. A little three-year-old girl has wandered into his path, and even this hardened, self-centered criminal is unwilling to run her down during his get-away. Joe is a despicable human being, yet compassion surfaces in his life.

Imagine another scene: A kind and gentle women by the name of Ginny is about to receive an award from a prestigious humanitarian group. Ginny has sacrificially given of her time, money, and energy in order to help unwed mothers find a life of dignity. On countless occasions she has patiently offered counsel to those who often did not appreciate her efforts. Many times, she has endured

---

1. Anthropology, from the Greek *anthropos*, i.e., man, is the study of human beings and what makes them what they are.

hostility and verbal abuse. Though it all, she gained a reputation for her tender tenacity and amazing calm amid even the most volatile circumstances. During a break in the awards program, Ginny excuses herself to go to the ladies' room. However, as she enters one of the stalls, she is startled by a women who flings open the stall door, practically knocking Ginny off of her feet. Ginny regains her balance but immediately swells with anger. Then, in an out-of-character moment, she curses the woman, embarrassing her in front of those who witnessed the mishap. Ginny is a genuinely kind human being, but this does render her impervious to rage.

These two imaginary scenes are illustrative of what it means to be human. But the lesson here is not merely that people display varying degrees of good and evil but that no one can avoid the best and worst features that comprise humanity.

John Calvin once wrote that "nearly all the wisdom we possess, that is to say, true and sound wisdom, consists in two parts: the knowledge of God and of ourselves."[2] From this perspective a study of the human condition is of paramount importance. Taking seriously the aforementioned positive and negative characteristics, and with a view to God and His Word, we will seek to identify and clarify those components that define who and what human beings a e.

Some, of course, seeing the darker side of humanity, will be quick to point out those aspects of mankind that are unseemly. Thus, man[3] is considered a monster of sorts, out of step with His Maker, and basically resistant to divine instruction. Others will just as quickly point out human virtues. After all, no one can claim to have rightly understood what it means to be human without recognizing man's great achievements and his uniqueness among God's creation.

While few would be willing to reduce mankind to either its best or worst elements, many, and perhaps most, *do* tend to emphasize one or the other of these attributes. When this occurs, those who make such judgments are liable to misdiagnose the human condition

---

2. John Calvin, *The Institutes of Christian Religion*, vol. 1, trans. Ford Lewis Battles (Philadelphia, PA.: The Westminster Press, MCMLX), 35.

3. For the sake of simplicity, the term "man" is employed throughout this paper, as are the masculine pronouns "he" and "him." The intention, however, is not to emphasize maleness nor to diminish femaleness. Rather, this terminology is a shorthand way of referring to the entire human race, both male and female.

and so react to their fellow man in inappropriate ways. Likewise, they are prone to misread their own hearts and lives.

A better approach recognizes that both dignity and depravity mark humanity, and that man cannot be properly perceived apart from this balance. Motivated by these concerns, this study begins with a brief survey of human history.

The Big Picture: Dignity and Depravity

The Bible begins with God's creative activity (Genesis 1-2). He is the architect and fashioner of all things, and what He makes is good. But the greatest feature of the creation is not the beautiful and boundless cosmos. Neither is it this magnificent planet. The Maker's masterpiece is man: "God created man in His own image, in the image of God He created him, male and female He created them" (Genesis 1:27).

Crafted in the divine image, humanity was imbued with great dignity. In a very real sense, man mirrored God. In limited though genuine ways, human beings resembled their Creator. It was therefore natural for the first humans to obey God and delight in His will. Man was a marvel to behold as he walked with his Lord.

Eventually, though, the creature rebelled against God. Instead of heeding the Creator's word, man chose his own path (Genesis 3:1ff). As a result, the human race was plunged into a state of moral and spiritual antipathy. Theologians often refer to this event (and the condition it yielded) as *the fall*.[4] Humanity not only became corrupt but passed on this corrupting principle, this tendency to reject the Author of all things. By turning on God, judgment came to the first humans and to all their posterity.

As history unfolded, man proved himself a strange mix of admirable and awful qualities. On the one hand, he was a spiritual insurrectionist, revolting against the divine will. In one passage of Scripture, this is described in terms of "suppress[ing] the truth in unrighteousness" (Romans 1:18). In another place human beings are said to be "darkened in their understanding" (Ephesians 4:18).

---

4. For a brief examination, see Robert Reymond, *A New Systematic Theology of the Christian Faith* (Nashville, TN: Thomas Nelson Publishers, 1998), 446-449.

John even declares that "men loved the darkness rather than the light"(John 3:19).

On the other hand, humanity was not completely given over to this corrupt nature. Due to the providential benefits of God and the remaining imprint of his Maker, man was still capable of noble aspirations and kind deeds. Though twisted and marred, God's image remained (Acts 17:29).

The portrait of mankind is puzzling. Clearly, man has scorned and turned against his Maker. Then again, there is still something in man, however buried by rebellious tendencies, that resonates with the divine. Indeed, this is what places humanity in such an absurd situation. While possessing a certain affinit for spiritual matters, human beings consistently resist any inclination to follow the true God, preferring idols (Romans 1:20-23; 1 Peter 4:3). Man does this not only by turning on God but by misusing and abusing the very gifts God placed within him (Romans 1:21). Plantinga describes this as "perverting special human excellencies."[5]

The story does not end here, however, for God would send His Son, Jesus the promised Messiah,[6] to rescue this fallen race (Galatians 4:4-5). Th ough the redemptive accomplishments of the Son of God, those united to Him by faith are forgiven their many wrongs (Ephesians 1:7; Romans 5:1; 8:1). Furthermore, the Spirit of God takes up special residence in them and begins to gradually shape them into the image of Jesus Himself (Galatians 5:22ff; Ephesians 2:10). This reshaping process will reach its goal when Jesus returns to earth; at that point, every believer will be utterly transformed (1 John 3:2).

Mankind's history is multi-faceted, beginning with beauty, turning to rebellion, consisting of a complex combination of good and evil, and (for believers) leading to perfection. As to man's current condition, it is evident that he is, in the words of Kreeft, "a living oxymoron: wretched greatness, great wretchedness, rational animal,

---

5. Cornelius Plantinga Jr., *Not the Way It's Supposed to Be: A Breviary of Sin* (Grand Rapids, MI: William B. Eerdmans Publishing Company, 1995), 3.

6. Messiah, which means "anointed one," is the term used to describe God's special messenger, who would come to deliver His people from spiritual slavery. It is the Hebrew equivalent of the Greek *Christos* or Christ.

mortal spirit, thinking reed."[7] Man is simultaneously corrupt and marvelous, depraved and dignified. Each of these categories aptly describes all human beings, and neither category can be neglected if we want to achieve a full-orbed view of humanity.

What Now?

If the above assessment is accurate, it will have a profound impact on the way we share the gospel. Since our *apologia* is aimed at people, it is essential that we know what they are like. A number of applications can be made.

1. *Any truly Christian apologetic takes into consideration both human depravity and human dignity.*

    Concerning anthropology, it is important that we refrain from allowing our biases and theological presuppositions to get in the way of discovering all that Scripture teaches about mankind. Even among those who know better, there is a tendency to give mere lip-service to a portion of the human equation, while emphasizing one's preferred aspect of the truth. Thus, human dignity is chosen over human depravity, or vice versa.[8]

    Of course no one comes to the Bible without some prior assumptions. Indeed, to the degree that one's presuppositions are built upon an accurate interpretation of Scripture, this is a good thing, and it would be ludicrous to suppose that one could drop all previous beliefs each time one comes to a biblical text. Still, whatever a person's current perspective on a topic or text, Scripture itself must remain at the center of his inquiries.

    > The riddle which divine revelation alone is able to unlock is that of the *misery* and the *nobility* of human-

---

7. Peter Kreeft, *Christianity for Modern Pagans: Pascal's Pensées Edited, Outlined and Explained* (San Francisco, CA: Ignatius Press, 1993), 55.

8. Some believers tend to overly emphasize human dignity by allowing secular versions of self-esteem and pop-psychology to dominate their thinking. Other believers are so focused on their human imperfections that they become introspective and depressed. Both extremes miss key facets of the human equation.

kind. Humans demonstrate baseness of all kinds (first and foremost moral and spiritual) and yet traits that witness to royal descent.⁹

An even-handed review of various biblical texts reveals that both of the categories mentioned here warrant acceptance. The efore, whatever the difficult in reconciling these seemingly opposite components, Scripture legitimizes both dignity and depravity as integral pieces of humanity's current situation. The task, then, is to rightly identify and balance them.

If human beings can be described in both positive and negative ways, it is only right to incorporate these elements into the way one views the world. To see only the beauty of man is to display naivete; this type of one-sidedness can lead to a minimizing of the awful predicament brought on by the Fall.

Then again, when only human frailty and impropriety are emphasized, it is difficul to avoid cynicism and shame. Taken to its extreme, this "everything is bad" or "everyone is evil" mentality can cause us to sever ties with the real world, losing our point of contact with those outside of the faith.

2. *A Christian apologetic must allows these truths to impact the doing of apologetics.*

Any apologetic that fails to recognize that we human beings are indeed fallen creatures will fall short of reaching others effectively. To expect that we can simply reason people into a relationship with God demonstrates that we either underestimate the hardheartedness of human beings (minimizing their tendency to ignore or flee from God's Word) or overestimate our ability to convince others of the truth (exaggerating our expertise and/or our power to change hearts).

On the other hand, if we accept the Scriptural portrayal of human beings, we will remain humble in our effo ts, recognizing that, valid as our effo ts might be, our *apologia* requires divine backing. Jesus once said, "apart from me you can do nothing"

---

9. Henri Blocher, *Original Sin: Illuminating the Riddle* (Grand Rapids, MI: William B. Eerdmans Publishing Company, 1997), 85.

(John15:5). Likewise, apart from God's intervention and assistance our *apologia* can do nothing.

Furthermore, any apologetic that doesn't take into account humanity's dignity will refrain from wholeheartedly engaging people. If God rescues people without our effo ts, there is no need to expend energy trying to do so. But, if we rightly perceive the wonder and beauty of human beings, we will exude compassion, desire their betterment, and diligently seek to do everything in our power to connect them with the One who gives good gifts and leads people to life.

3. *Our perspective on humanity, which is derived from Scripture, must be continually coupled with the real life perspective we gain through interaction with people.*

It is important, in other words, to allow our attitudes about human beings to be shaped in both theoretical and practical ways. Our theory of anthropology is located in Scripture, which provides insight into the nature of humanity. But the theoretical must be complemented by the experiential if we are going to both apply Scripture appropriately (and not merely hypothesize about it) and remain open to the change that comes through further research.

To be clear, Scripture holds an authority that is greater than our mere experiences of the world. Just because we "feel" a certain way about something does not give us the right to ignore or violate what Scripture explicitly teaches. In this sense Scripture is the final ba ometer on those matters to which it speaks.

That said, it is also true that God operates in the world, and He is certainly able to teach us various things through our experiences with people in the world. It is possible that what we encounter in our lives will cause us to reexamine and perhaps tweak our current views. In this sense our experiences with people can cause us to reassess our interpretations and theological assumptions. Sometimes, this evaluative process leads to a confirmation of current views. Other times, our reexamination of Scripture reveals insights that were previously minimized or missed.

Perhaps, an example will help to clarify these matters. Some time ago, I was studying the subject of human depravity. Along the way, I located many passages of Scripture that validated this general outlook (e.g., 1 Corinthians 2:14; Romans 9:9-20; Ephesians 2:1-5). Likewise, as I looked around, my view of human defectiveness was confirmed by my observations. Scripture taught that human beings are corrupt, and I noticed this corruption.

At one point, however, I happened to run into a number of people who, though not believers, demonstrated some impressive moral qualities. Given their sincerity and the undeniable reality of their kind acts, I began to recognize that there was something about men and women that my current perspective didn't fully take into account. My views were mostly governed by the negative passages of Scripture, those that (accurately) described human rebellion. But, as I discovered, I needed to balance these thoughts with other equally valid Scriptural claims. My experiences compelled me to reexamine Scripture, enabling me to recognize that human depravity must be balanced by human dignity. Though I had always given lip service to the positive features of mankind, I had not allowed Scripture itself to shape my attitudes (Genesis 1:27; Acts 17:29; James 3:9). My experience of humanity's better characteristics actually chased me back to Scripture where I was able to gather new anthropological insights and a more accurate perspective.

While Scripture is to hold sway in our lives and in the way we approach truth, our experiences of God and His world can be an avenue by which we grow, both theologically and personally. The point is that our views of humanity, derived from God's Word, must be taken into society. Only then will we achieve a humble balance, and only then will the ideas we believe actually impact the world in which we live.

Conclusion

"What is man?" is one of the most important questions one can ask, and one of the most difficul to adequately answer. Indeed, the desire to understand human beings is limited by personal biases and an incomplete perception of God's mind in Scripture.

This does not mean, however, that we are left in the dark, for both experience of God's world and a study of God's Word reveal that there is a bright and a dark side to humanity. A biblical worldview addresses these realities.

Yet, these positive and negative depictions of man are much more that theoretical ideas, as Lewis marvelously captures:

> It is a serious thing to live in a society of possible gods and goddesses, to remember that the dullest and most uninteresting person you can talk to may one day be a creature which, if you saw it now, you would be strongly tempted to worship, or else a horror and a corruption such as you now meet, if at all, only in a nightmare.[10]

These anthropological reflections challenge us to prayerfully consider the manner in which we approach apologetics. To the extent that we recognize human limitations and shortcomings (our own and in others), and with an equal realization of the Creator's grand design as reflected in human beings, our responsibility is to share our *apologia*, and indeed our lives, with those who come our way.

---

10. C. S. Lewis, *The Weight of Glory* (New York: HarperCollins Publishers Inc., 2001), 45.

> "The Christian is called to be a pilgrim,
> a learner to the end of her days.
> But she knows the way."

Lesslie Newbigin

> "I have become all things to all men,
> so that I may by all means save some."

1 Corinthians 9:22

We are living in an increasingly post-Christian society, and many pundits have offered their suggestions for meeting today's challenges.

Those of a more traditional bent expend much energy trying to coax people, and society in general, in a Christian direction. Clearly, there is something to be gained from our efforts to recapture "the good old days."

At the same time, we mustn't sit around merely complaining about the worst trends in society when our primary duty is to meet people where they are. This is what Jesus did, and it is also what is advocated by Paul in Acts 17. In this passage we find a paradigm for engaging non-Christian people and society.

Chapter Four

The Athenian Challenge

Communicating the Gospel in Non-Christian Society

"Truly, truly, I say to you, unless one is born again he cannot see the kingdom of God" (John 3:3)

"For God so loved the world, that He gave His only begotten Son, that whoever believes in Him shall not perish but have eternal life" (John 3:16).

"For the wages of sin is death, but the free gift of God is eternal life in Christ Jesus our Lord" (Romans 6:23).

"The time is fulfilled, and the kingdom of God is at hand; repent and believe in the gospel" (Mark 1:15).

"Believe in the Lord Jesus, and you will be saved" (Acts 16:31).

These and many other biblical passages are often quoted by Christians when evangelizing, and there is little doubt why. They convey important realities about God, man, and the way in which humanity can be brought into a right standing before its

Creator. Indeed, spiritually deficient human beings desperately need to hear the words that lead to eternal life. One of the believer's greatest responsibilities, therefore, is to share these truths with others.

When the recipients of the Christian message are relatively familiar with the Bible's story-line, the communication of the gospel can move forward in a rather straightforward fashion. Whatever obstacles impede evangelistic success, at least the language barrier is fairly minimal. The exchange of ideas is greatly simplified when Christians and non-Christians hold to very similar worldviews.

However, not all people share the same assumptions. Missionaries, long realizing this fact, have expended great amounts of energy bridging language and cultural gaps, seeking to speak God's Word to people who are unaware of its meaning. But one need not travel to a foreign land to experience this phenomenon, for many people in the Western world are equally unaware of Christian truth.

There was a time, not long ago, when much of society was influenced by a Judeo-Christian perspective. Christmas carols were well-known. Sin was a generally understood concept. God was viewed in basically biblical terms. While many people still take pride in their religious (even Christian) heritage, the fact remains that a large percentage of today's population is biblically illiterate.

The truths many believers take for granted are quite foreign to non-Christians. Carson illustrates this point: "One of my students commented . . . that he was walking in Chicago with his girlfriend, who had a wooden cross hanging from a chain around her neck. A lad stopped her on the sidewalk and asked why she had a plus sign for a necklace."[1] It is not an exaggeration to say that the world has undergone something of a paradigm shift.

Unfortunately, many believers have not properly responded to these societal changes. As a result, certain segments of the church compromise the Bible's message, hoping to make Christianity more palatable to the consumer. At the other extreme, some retreat into the fortress of their own ecclesiastical communities; though still believing in evangelism, they insist on forcing the world into a cultur-

---

1. D. A. Carson, "Athens Revisited" in *Telling the Truth: Evangelizing Postmoderns*, ed. D. A. Carson (Grand Rapids, MI.: Zondervan Publishing House, 2000), 385.

ally outdated grid.² Consequently, both frustration and arrogance abound. Frustration occurs when those who sincerely desire to share the gospel lack the biblical and cultural know-how to do so effectively. On the other hand, arrogance is the fruit of ministries that spend an inordinate amount of time criticizing and separating from others, without also putting forth every effo t to reach them. While these characterizations may be somewhat rigid, and though there are surely a good number of exceptions, the fact remains that many believers are out-of-touch when it comes to sharing the gospel in a primarily non-Christian environment.³

It is thus with good reason that the biblical writers address this subject. Among a number of important texts, none is more relevant than Acts 17:16-34. This passage will be the focus of this present study. The goal will be to uncover and apply truths that are relevant to the promulgation of the gospel in a neo-pagan⁴ world.

Survey

¹⁶Now while Paul was waiting for them at Athens, his spirit was being provoked within him as he was observing the city full of idols. ¹⁷So he was reasoning in the synagogue with the Jews and the God-fearing Gentiles, and in the market place every day with those who happened to be present. ¹⁸And also some of the Epicurean and Stoic philosophers were conversing with him. Some were saying, "What would this idle babbler wish to say?" Others, "He seems to be a proclaimer of strange deities," – because he was preaching Jesus and the resurrection. ¹⁹And they

---

2. For example many Christians maintain cultural preferences that are out of sync with contemporary forms. Though these issues can often be complicated and controversial, the fact remains that some within the church are governed more by ecclesiastic comfort zones, their traditions, than they are by the truth. It is sad to see believers missing out on genuine opportunities to assist others because of an unwillingness to bend in areas that are a matter of personal freedom.

3. George Barna, *The Second Coming of the Church* (Nashville, TN.: Word Publishing, 1998), 15-28.

4. *Pagan* is used here not primarily as a point of criticism but to delineate those who lack a connection with a Judeo-Christian worldview and its accompanying language and concepts.

took him and brought him to the Areopagus, saying, "May we know what this new teaching is which you are proclaiming? [20]For you are bringing some strange things to our ears; so we want to know what these things mean." [21](Now all the Athenians and the strangers visiting there used to spend their time in nothing other than telling or hearing something new.) [22]So Paul stood in the midst of the Areopagus and said, "Men of Athens, I observe that you are very religious in all respects. [23]For while I was passing through and examining the objects of your worship, I also found an altar with this inscription, 'TO AN UNKNOWN GOD.' The efore what you worship in ignorance, this I proclaim to you. [24]The God who made the world and all things in it, since He is Lord of heaven and earth, does not dwell in temples made with hands; [25]nor is He served by human hands, as though He needed anything, since He himself gives to all people life and breath and all things; [26]And He made from one man every nation of mankind to live on the face of the earth, having determined their appointed times and the boundaries of their habitation, [27]That they would seek God, if perhaps they might grope for Him and find Him, though He is not far from each one of us; [28]for in Him we live and move and exist, as even some of your own poets have said, 'For we also are His children.' [29]Being then the children of God, we ought not to think that the Divine Nature is like gold or silver or stone, an image formed by the art and thought of man. [30]The efore having overlooked the times of ignorance, God is now declaring to men that all people everywhere should repent, [31]because He has fi ed a day in which He will judge the world in righteousness through a Man whom He has appointed, having furnished proof to all men by raising Him from the dead." [32]Now when they heard of the resurrection from the dead, some began to sneer, but others said, "We shall hear you again concerning this." [33]So Paul went out of their midst. [34]But some men joined him and believed, among who also were Dionysius the Aeropagite and a women named Damaris and others with them.

Paul's missionary journeys took him to many places throughout the ancient world. In his travels he often encountered resistance to the message he preached. On one particular occasion, he was forced to leave Thessalonica, fleeing for his life (Acts 17:5-10a).[5] From there he stopped at Berea (10b-15) before having to leave that city as well. Then, in God's providence, he wound up in Athens, which was a metropolis of pagan culture and thought.

Upon arriving in Athens, Paul was immediately struck by the rank idolatry of the city. Luke says that "his spirit was being provoked within him" (16). But the apostle would not be deterred from his mission. Indeed, the sad condition of Athens seemed to spur him on as he began to share the Christian gospel. The spectacle of a city so entirely dedicated to false worship stirred him to the conviction that here, if anywhere, were men and women who sorely needed the gospel with which he had been entrusted."[6]

As usual, Paul followed his practice of reaching out first to the Jews and God-fearers[7] in the synagogue (17). Then, he moved to the market place and conversed with the common people (17). At one point, he encountered Epicurean and Stoic philosophers (18). Some of these mocked,[8] but others were curious about the apostle's words.

---

5. Since this section is based on Acts Chapter 17, and because the majority of passages will be taken from this chapter, references to verses within it shall not include the name of the book nor the chapter. All other biblical references will follow the form of book name, chapter, and verse.

6. F. F. Bruce, *The Book of Acts* , NICNT (Grand Rapids, MI.: William B. Eerdmans Publishing Company, 1988), 329.

7. Concerning the designation "God-fearers," Hemer notes that "there were at least in some places numbers of Gentiles who were close enough to Judaism to be considered part of the community, albeit a separate part, without becoming full proselytes." Colin J. Hemer, *The Book of Acts in the Setting of Hellenistic History* (Winona Lake, IN.: Eisenbrauns, 1990), 447.

8. Part of the Athenians' initial confusion may have been due to a misunderstanding of Paul's words. "Apparently they misconstrued his message to be about two deities, Jesus and his consort, Anastasis (the Greek word for resurrection), understanding them perhaps as Healing (Jesus sounds something like this in Greek) and Restoration." David J. Williams, *Acts* (Peabody, MA.: Hendrickson Publishers, 1990), 303. Also, see John R. W. Stott, *The Message of Acts* (Downers Grove, IL.: InterVarsity Press, 1990), 282.

This led to an opportunity to stand before the Areopagus, that "most venerable Athenian court,"[9] and clarify his teaching (19ff) [10]

Paul's speech is a masterpiece of cross-cultural communication. He begins by acknowledging the Athenian's religious nature, drawing attention to an altar on which was engraved "to an unknown God" (17:23). This practice might be a result of pagan apprehension in the face of unknown forces. Various deities needed to be appeased, including those that were not known.[11] At any rate, this altar is an admission of the Athenian's ignorance.

By way of contrast, the living God is not limited to human conceptions of Him (24-25, 29). Rather, as the transcendent Creator (26-28), He is independent of any creature (25). Quoting from their own poets, the apostle drives home a point the Athenians should have recognized. As divine image bearers, they ought to have perceived the foolishness of trying to manufacture deities (28-29).

But, according to Paul, God is not aloof and uninterested in mankind. Not only does He transcend His creation, He is also present within it (27). Furthermore, He has arranged history in such a way that people would seek after Him (27). The true God, the God who can be known, has been patient in His dealings with the uninformed (30). This is precisely why lost humans must turn from their ignorance and rebellion, looking to God's appointed mediator, "a Man whom He has appointed, having furnished proof to all men by raising Him from the dead" (31).

As might be expected, there were a number of responses to the apostle's announcement of the resurrection. Some sneered, being unable or unwilling to crawl outside of their own pagan presuppositions (32). Others wanted to hear more (32). Eventually, some believed (34).

---

9. F. F. Bruce, *The Acts of the Apostles: The Greek Text with Introduction and Commentary* (Grand Rapids, MI.: William B. Eerdmans Publishing Company, 1990), 378.

10. "Αρειος πάγος : the two-word form, applied to the court, is regularly used in many inscriptions of the period. This hearing probably took place before the court in its meeting-place in the Agora, not on the actual hill so called." Hemer, *Acts*, 117.

11. Carson, *The Gagging of God*, 499.

In summary Acts 17:16-34 reveals how Paul made use of the Athenian's own admissions, experiences, and writings in his quest to lead them away from idolatry and into a relationship with the true and living God. Clearly, Paul's encounter with ancient Athenian pagans has great evangelistic and apologetic relevance for similar situations today.

Apologetic Precursors

Before proceeding, it will be helpful to reflect on some of the key ideas that influenced the apostle Paul's approach. These were of course already a part of his mind-set, and they can be observed in many other portions of the New Testament. However, a number of factors are particularly evident here in Acts 17. In seeking to reach the Athenians with the gospel, certain truths helped inform and guide Paul's effo ts. Among these are the following:

Theological Factors

Theologicall , Paul's thoughts were governed by God's revealed will (2 Timothy 3:16-17). The Old Testament Scriptures, coupled with the revelation received from the risen Christ, shaped his views. His understanding of God is evident here in this Athenian address. God is depicted as the Creator "who made the world and all things in it" (24); pantheism is clearly ruled out. Paul goes on to say that God is sovereign and so not limited in any way (25). This is sometimes referred to as divine aseity, which means that God is a self-existent being who is completely independent of His creation.[12] Rather than needing man, humanity actually needs Him. At the same time, however, this One who transcends human beings is "not far from each one of us" (27). That is, He is "present in, close to and involved with creation."[13] God is immanent.

The portrait painted by Paul is of a magnificent deity. On the one hand, He defies human grasp and categorization. On the other hand, He is the God who relates to His people, the knowable Lord

---

12. Carson, *Telling the Truth*, 392.
13. Stanley J. Grenz, J. David Guretzki, and Cherith Fee Nordling, "Immanence" in *Pocket Dictionary of Theological Terms* (Downers Grove, IL.: InterVarsity Press, 1999), 63.

whose very acts of forbearance are a call to repentance. Paul believed in and proclaimed a God who is transcendent beyond human comprehension, yet closer than anyone can imagine.

Anthropological Factors

A number of truths about man are evident in Acts 17. Two points are particularly significant. First, humanity apart from divine revelation is ignorant and idolatrous. The Athenian's ignorance is implied in their altars which were inscribed "to an unknown god." By their own admission, they were uninformed. Therefore, the gods they *did* honor were misrepresentations of the one true God. In essence a lack of special revelation left them to themselves. Apart from divine aid, they could not escape their blindness and misapprehension. This is why they took to idolatry, the making of false deities.[14] All of this placed them in a precarious position, separated from the true God and culpable for their darkened state, willful rebellion, and vain worship.

Second, communication amid paganism is not completely closed-off. Though it is not his emphasis, Paul insists that even these pagans were aware of certain basic facts about God. They were at least cognizant of their own ignorance, hence their acknowledgment of an unknown god. Furthermore, their writers had alluded to the very things Paul declares. "In Him we live and move and exist" possibly originated with Epimenides (28), while "For we also are His children" (28) is often attributed to Aratus, a stoic poet.[15] Thus, "glimmerings of truth, insights from general revelation, may be found in

---

14. For more on this subject, see P. W. Comfort, "Idolatry" in *The Dictionary of Paul and His Letters* (Downers Grove, IL.: InterVarsity Press, 1993), 424-426.

15. See Hemer, *Acts* , 118 and Bruce, Acts: Greek , 384-385. The words attributed to Aratus, who possibly borrowed them from an earlier writer named Cleanthes, refer to Zeus, not to the true God. Still, this language mirrors a biblical truth. The point is not that all human beings are God's children in a redemptive sense but that they are His by creation. Therefore, fallen humanity has an intuitive awareness of certain things, not the least of which is the absurdity of thinking "that the Divine Nature is like gold or silver or stone" (29).

non-Christian authors."[16] Or, as Mayers puts it, "man, groping in God's universe, can 'feel' and vaguely approximate the truth."[17]

Paul's anthropology consisted of these elements: (1) Human beings are ignorant and culpable creatures who naturally allow their own machinations to draw them away from God and into God-dishonoring choices. Because of human depravity, man requires both special revelation and spiritual intervention. (2) Man is a divine-image bearer who can perceive the shadows of divine realities. As a result, he can be reasoned with (17), in the hope that God might change the heart of those who are presently misled (30ff). Indeed, the detrimental effects resulting from the "one man" (26), Adam, can only be reversed by another man, God's chosen "Man" (31), Jesus, who is able to guide fallen humanity back to its Maker.

Christological Factors

While in Athens, Paul is especially concerned to provide the context within which the Christian gospel is coherent. He therefore spends a good amount of time dealing with larger worldview issues before proceeding to the topic of Jesus Himself. Yet, none of this should lead the reader to dismiss the relevance of what Paul does say about God's Son.

For one, it is evident that Paul's reasoning is purposeful and directed. Not only does he lay out a biblical worldview, but he does so in order to lead people specifically to Jesus. That is, the whole aim of the apostle's effo ts is Christological. At the very least, this shows that Paul viewed Jesus as the goal of his evangelism. No priority was higher than pointing people to the Son of God (1 Corinthians 2:2; Galatians 6:14; Philippians 1:21).

Paul's high view of Christ is evident in many places (Philippians 2:5-11; Colossians 1:15-20). Here in Acts 17, some of Jesus' qualifi cations are mentioned. The apostle speaks of Jesus in exalted terms. For instance, He is the "appointed judge," the very one who will take center-stage when the eschatological judgment ensues. As such, He is

---

16. Stott, *The Message of Acts*, 286.
17. Mayers, *Balanced Apologetics*, 166.

to be both revered (because of His role as Judge) and embraced (since He is the One through whom salvation comes).[18]

Of course anyone can make extravagant claims. What makes Jesus unique, among other things, is the fact that He received God's approval.

> The proof Paul offers to establish his argument is Jesus' resurrection. . . . The resurrection is . . . the linchpin for . . . applying the death and resurrection of Christ to one's eternal destiny. It establishes both the warning of judgment and the promise of salvation blessings.[19]

Jesus is the Lord of the eschaton, the one endorsed by God, the risen Savior, and the unique Judge. This is why the strategy Paul employs here, whatever its many nuances, is distinctly gospel oriented. Steering people toward Jesus, the resurrected Savior, the one with impeccable credentials, is the apostle's chief aim.

Priorities and Praxis

The city of Athens was (and is) a marvel to behold, its magnificent sculptures and architecture bearing witness to a noble history. Indeed, there is little doubt that Paul, a cultured man himself, would have been able to appreciate its great feats of architecture.

> [The] buildings and monuments . . . were unrivaled. The acropolis, the town's ancient citadel, which was elevated enough to be seen for miles around, has been described as "one vast composition and architecture and sculpture dedicated to the national glory and to the worship of the gods."[20]

Yet, for all its captivating beauty, Luke reports of Paul that "his spirit was being provoked within him" (16). Rather than being distracted

---

18. Note Luke's mention that some believed (34). Obviously, this belief is in something. In Christian usage this has to include at least some knowledge of Jesus as Savior. Thus, it is likely that aul touched on this subject.

19. William J. Larkin Jr., *Acts* (Downers Grove, IL.: InterVarsity Press, 1995), 260.

20. Stott, *Acts*, 277.

by the city's splendors, he immediately recognized that beneath the surface lay an odious idolatry. Larkin notes:

> Paul is more than greatly distressed, for he experiences a paroxysm in his spirit, a provocation of anger or grief or both, because the glory due to God alone is being given to idols. The Lord reacted the same way to idolatry in Israel (Deut 9:7, 18, 22; Ps 106:28-29; Is 65:2-3; compare Is 42:8), and so should we.[21]

Paul's zeal for God's glory would not allow him to ignore the blasphemy of this idolatrous city. Just as God had been provoked to anger by the idolatry of ancient Israel (Isaiah 65:2-3), so Paul was incensed by what he saw in Athens. It is not that he put on a pompous show of disapproval, as if that would accomplish anything. Nor did Paul view himself as "a cut above" his fellow human beings. Rather, he experienced a great inner unrest. God deserves unrivaled allegiance and is jealous when that allegiance is transferred to anyone or anything else; believers are to share this outlook.

Christians are to view all of life from the perspective of their Lord. When He is dishonored or minimized, when someone or something usurps His position, those who know Him ought to be appropriately appalled. Though believers should be careful, as Paul was, not to unnecessarily offend others, it is also essential to recognize the dark character (as well as the sadness) of a defective worldview. The honor of God must reign paramount in any efforts to reach others with the gospel.

> It is not only the comprehensiveness of Paul's message in Athens which is impressive . . . but also the depth and power of his motivation. Why is it that, in spite of the great needs and opportunities of our day, the church slumbers peacefully on, and that so many Christians are deaf and dumb, deaf to Christ's commission and tongue-tied in testimony? I think the major reason is this: we do not speak as Paul spoke because we do not feel as Paul felt. . . . For he saw men and women, created by God in the image of God, giving to idols the homage which was due to him alone. . . . Paul was deeply pained by the

---

21. Larkin, *Acts*, 251-252.

idolatrous city of Athens. Have we been provoked by the idolatrous cities of the contemporary world?[22]

But Paul did more than contemplate the unsettling realities of Athens, for he was compelled to reach out to these people. It is instructive to observe Paul's actions. He started in the synagogue where he spoke to the biblically-informed people of that community, those somewhat acquainted with the Old Testament Scriptures. Then, he moved on to the market place, the so-called agora. Finally, he addressed the intellectuals, first presumably in the agora, and then in a more formal setting. One can only marvel at Paul's flexibilit . He made inroads where he could, took advantage of opportunities, and spoke with all kinds of people.

Though the level of understanding and education surely varied among his hearers, the apostle consistently reasoned with them (17).

> The duty of Christian witness involves reasoning, as the descriptions of Paul's missionary activity show. Faith is not created by reasoning, but neither is it created without it. The e is more involved in witness to Christ than throwing pre-arranged clumps of texts at unbelieving heads; the meaning and application of the gospel must be explained to men and women in terms of their actual situation. This equires hard thinking.[23]

To reason is to discuss a point of view, to appeal to the logic and coherence of a position, to intelligently show forth the inner consistency and attractiveness of something. In essence, apologetics seeks to explain why a person ought to embrace the truth. With God's revealed will as the basis and Jesus as the aim (18), Paul did more than simply state a position or announce that Jesus is Lord; Paul made use of reasoned proclamation and discussion.[24]

---

22. Stott, *Acts*, 290-291.

23. J. I. Packer, *Fundamentalism and the Word of God* (Grand Rapids, MI.: William B. Eerdmans Publishing Company, 1988), 135-136.

24. The point, of course, is not that reason is the only avenue of discovery. Nor, when one reasons, is this limited to deep academic arguments. In view, rather, are the very human qualities of thinking, discussing, debating, and pondering. To reason, therefore, is to vigorously challenge people to consider the benefits of embracing the living od.

Perspectives on Apologetics

Having surveyed and extracted pertinent data from this key passage, including both theoretical and practical truths, it is now possible to delineate a number of relevant perspectives. Successful communication of the Christian gospel in a pagan or neo-pagan environment is facilitated by the appropriation and application of this Athenian paradigm. The following observations are intended to assist in the task of reaching out to the biblically uninformed.

1. *Interactive Apologetics: Good apologists engage the world in which they live.*

   One ingredient of evangelistic relevance is the ability of Christians to know something about their world. While successful witnessing has always depended on an awareness of one's social setting, today's situation represents a special challenge. The reason for this is quite simple; many contemporary believers operate in a cultural environment far removed from secular society.[25] This means that Christians must make a concerted effo t to become acquainted with the habits of contemporary men and women.

   The apostle Paul was a master of this approach. When in Athens, he observed the surroundings in order to familiarize himself with Athenian culture. Indeed, he apparently already possessed an understanding of pagan literature, as evidenced by his quoting their poets (17:28).

   > Summing up Paul's rhetorical strategy in Athens, we may note that the apostle was knowledgeable, dialectical, well-read, relevant, and rhetorically skillful. What particularly strikes the reader is his ability to

---

25. This is not meant to imply that all believers are completely lacking in contact with the secular world. However, for a variety of reasons, it is quite common for this contact to be quite shallow, and for Christians to take lightly the views of their non-Christian acquaintances. For a better alternative, see Dick Staub, *Too Christian, Too Pagan* (Grand Rapids, MI.: Zondervan Publishing House, 2000), 61-67.

accommodate himself to the knowledge base of most Athenians.[26]

In other words Paul lived in the real world and knew how people thought and lived. In like manner believers who live in today's neo-pagan society must interact with it. The trends, popular ideas, current styles, and cultural assumptions of the day must be grasped. This type of cultural awareness is fostered by reading the newspaper, watching television, surfing the internet, and a host of other ways.[27] It is not that believers should stand on the periphery of society, performing cold cultural analysis. Rather, they are to live within the "walls" of society, daily (and prayerfully) befriending all kinds of people. "If you want to build bridges to any culture, you need to be an observer of it. That means being inside it"[28]

Now, this entire project raises important questions about how we ought to relate to the world.[29] While believers are not to emulate the anti-God and idolatrous attitudes that are present within every society, and though they are to be careful not to allow "the cares of this world" (Mark 4:7, 18-19) to take priority in their lives, Scripture endorses a type of "worldly" apologetic. Like Paul, and Jesus before Him (Luke 19:1-10), the apologetically-minded individual must spend quality time with the people of this generation. "If we do not take seriously the responsibility to build redemptive relationships with the lost, who will? Seeking such relationships should surely fig

---

26. J. Daryl Charles, "Engaging the (Neo) Pagan Mind: Paul's Encounter with Athenian Culture as a Model for CulturalApologetics" in *The Gospel and Contemporary Perspectives: Viewpoints from the Trinity Journal*, ed. Douglas Moo (Grand Rapids, MI.: Kregel Publications, 1997), 136.

27. For some excellent suggestions on becoming culturally literate, see Staub, *Too Christian, Too Pagan*, 129-165.

28. Michael Green and Alister McGrath, *How Shall We Reach Them? Defending and Communicating the Christian Faith to Nonbelievers* (Nashville, TN.: Thomas elson Publishers, 1995), 56.

29. [73]For a popular treatment of these issues, see Staub, *Too Christian, Too Pagan* , 33-67.

ure prominently into our personal and church philosophy of ministry."³⁰

Of course the only legitimate motive in one's effo ts to be culturally literate is love. "If you truly desire to be more effecti e taking Jesus into your world, one of the best places to start is to simply be the kind of friend Jesus is. And Jesus is a friend for sinners."³¹

2. *Worldview Apologetics: Good apologists provide the context, the biblical worldview, apart from which the gospel is unintelligible.*

Those who are culture watchers are keenly aware of the fact that the direction of society is often contrary to the biblical norm. Indeed, the assumptions and priorities of the contemporary world are often the antithesis of those found in Scripture.

This being the case, it is necessary to communicate Christian presuppositions. It is not enough to proclaim, "Jesus saves." As true as this statement is, it requires context. Before the Christian gospel can be perceived, a larger framework must be established. In other words it is important to help others comprehend the wider context within which "Jesus saves" is not only coherent but compelling.

As Paul seeks to communicate with the Athenians, a number of truths come to the fore. Basically, he is concerned to share something about God, humanity, and Jesus. God, Paul says, is the transcendent, immanent Creator (24-29). He is both the sovereign Judge to whom all must give an account (26, 31) and the compassionate Lord who graciously invites people into His presence (27, 30). Humanity, as the apostle explains, is both ignorant and culpable (23ff) but also retains a vestigial awareness of God (Romans 1:18-22). Paul shares these facts with the Athenians in order that they might understand both their true hope and their need to change.

---

30. Tom Hovestol, *Extreme Righteousness: Seeing Ourselves in the Pharisees* (Chicago, IL.: Moody Press, 1997), 150.

31. Staub, *Too Christian, Too Pagan*, 51.

Only after laying out these broad strokes does he turn explicitly to the subject of Jesus.[32] When Jesus' name is finally mentioned, the apostle shares information about His status. To this end, God declared Jesus the eschatological Judge, which God demonstrated by raising Jesus from the dead (31). While many of the pagans of Paul's day would have balked (and in fact did, 32) at his explanation, it was nonetheless necessary to point out that God had furnished cogent evidence for all who cared to see.[33]

In the final analysis, the Areopagus speech is a brilliant attempt to disclose true ideas to those who had little understanding of (or liking for) the Christian gospel. It entails both the correction of commonly held yet erroneous views and the communication of God's true ways. If contemporary apologists are to follow this pattern, they too must determine to speak not only about Jesus but about the wider biblical story-line. In other words it will be essential to have a firm grasp of the biblical worldview, for only then will the message of the cross and resurrection make sense to contemporary men and women.

3. *Contextualized Apologetics: Good apologists communicate in culturally sensitive ways.*

It has been suggested that Christians should know something about the world in which they live, and they must then seek to provide a broader framework for those who are unaware of the truth. Next, it is important to recognize the manner in which

---

32. It can certainly be argued that the name of Jesus had already been introduced in Paul's earlier witness (18). True enough. However, this does not detract from the apostle's basic plan, which was to ground his presentation of Jesus in the context of a wider biblical perspective. The point here is not that the name of Jesus is to be avoided, but that the gospel makes more sense to those who possess at least a rudimentary understanding of Scripture's story line.

33. At this point, some might ask why the apostle delved into the controversial subject of the resurrection. After all, the Athenians hardly took such talk seriously. Of course the resurrection must eventually be proclaimed because it is a fundamental tenet of the faith. But, it is especially important to recognize Paul's strategy here. He is not merely communicating facts about the resurrection, facts that made no sense in pagan thought. Rather, he hopes by first establishing a biblical worldview to get the Athenians to interpret the resurrection within the context of special revelation. Paul is trying primarily to get them to see this doctrine through Christian lenses.

the Christian worldview is to be communicated. In short, the subject of contextualization must be addressed.

"Contextualization occurs when the presentation and outworking of the gospel is done in a manner appropriate to the context in which it is found."[34] Thus, it involves the melding of the two previous principles. If a person understands his culture (principle # 1) and desires to provide a framework for understanding the gospel within that culture (principle # 2), it makes sense to do so in an appropriate manner.

A part of Paul's strategy involves finding areas of agreement with his hearers. Not only is he concerned to know his audience, but he looks for common ground. In Athens, for instance, he was able to glean truths from the Athenians' own writers and use these to point people to Jesus. As Paul speaks before the Areopagus, "the vocabulary is linguistically appropriate to his hearers, but at the level of the sentence and the paragraph, Paul in his report is saying just what he wants to say; he is establishing a biblical worldview."[35] Charles adds: "The striking significance of Acts 17:16-34 is the ability of Paul to clothe biblical revelation in a cultured and relevant argument to his pagan contemporaries."[36]

Believers today would do well to follow the apostle's example. It is not only important to be acquainted with cultural tendencies, but we must also shape our message to fit the contemporary scene. The truth is to be uncompromisingly and wisely enculturated.

4. *Teleological*[37] *Apologetics: Good apologists seek to direct people—wisely, gradually, and creatively—to the God who has revealed Himself through Jesus Christ.*

One danger of apologetic engagement is the tendency to deal merely in the abstract and theoretical. When this happens, top

---

34. Ajith Fernando, Acts, *The NIV Application Commentary* (Grand Rapids, MI.: Zondervan Publishing House, 1998), 480.
35. Carson, *Telling The Truth*, 392.
36. Charles, *The Gospel and Contemporary Perspectives*, 132.
37. Teleological comes from the Greek term *telos*, meaning purpose or end.

priority is given to winning the argument, or at least silencing critics. The problem with this model, however, is that it neglects the goal of apologetics, which is to unite fallen human beings with their Creator. While it is certainly proper to engage in serious doctrinal and theological study, the purpose of these things is to lead people to a knowledge of God.

On this score Paul's wisdom is once again evident. His effo t to communicate a biblical worldview in culturally relevant ways had as its aim the actual conversion of individuals. It was not enough to simply find a point of contact with ancient pagans or to share broad ideas with them. Rather, he actually called men and women to turn *to* God. All people must respond personally to the message of the gospel.

> [The] movement of a faithful apologetic is always in the direction of moral accountability. By underscoring the reality of future judgment, the apostle dismantles religious inclusivity: all people everywhere must repent and confront the knowledge of the Creator that has been imparted to them.[38]

But conversion is not merely an idea. It relates to a person, Jesus. This explains the direction of Paul's message. People must turn from their ways and look to this One whom God appointed. All of the groundwork Paul provides, all of the worldview apologetics, has a *telos*, an aim. That aim is that needy human beings would turn from their ways and embrace God's one-and-only Son. Hence, the need for teleological apologetics.

Conclusion

Paul's Athenian address represents a great challenge to contemporary apologists. The challenge is to understand this passage and then apply it to today's world. Basically, this starts with a proper biblical perspective, i.e., a correct understanding of Scripture and a corresponding commitment to the God therein revealed.

---

38. Charles, *The Gospel and Contemporary Perspectives*, 137.

With a right biblical and theological foundation, it is then possible to implement sound apologetic truths. These include connecting with the non-Christian world, communicating a biblical worldview, exuding cultural sensitivity, and aiming at conversion. Charles nicely summarizes:

> The Christian community must understand the culture in which it has been placed by the sovereign Lord. By demonstrating an understanding of culture, it is then able to engage culture with a measure of credibility. Finally, having humbly sought to be a student of and active participant in culture, the church is able to confront the false values that are lodged within culture. Perception, engagement, confrontation necessarily follow–in this order.[39]

Larkin adds: "We must reintroduce post-Christians to Jesus with freshness, without resorting to the traditional formulations they will call the 'old, old story.' But we must do so with faithfulness, telling it the way it was and is."[40] Our success in this endeavor will hinge greatly on our ability to understand and embody such passages as the one we have examined. Acts 17:16-34 provides incentive for communicating the good news in a pluralistic world, for reaching those with little access to a Christian worldview. What we do with this paradigm is the Athenian challenge.

---

39. Ibid., 136.
40. Larkin, *Acts*, 253.

Excursus:
Did Paul Fail and/or Compromise in Athens?

Paul wrote in 1 Corinthians 2:2 that he "determined to know nothing . . . except Jesus Christ and Him crucified." Because his work among the Corinthians (Acts 18) follows immediately on the heels of his ministry in Athens (Acts 17), some have speculated that these words are the apostle's way of rejecting the type of approach he utilized among the Athenians. Paul, it is said, realized the error of his ways and the foolishness of trying to reason with these pagans as he did. In essence he came to see that the Athenian address was little more than an act of compromise, a deficient and gospel-lacking effort to reach the inhabitants of that city.

In response to this suggestion, a number of points need to be mentioned. First, it is important to realize that what we possess here is a summary of a lengthier speech.[1] Luke merely provides the broad strokes of Paul's message. If we possessed the entire message, it is likely that we would glean additional information. Second, it is worth noting that the apostle may have been cut-off before he had concluded his speech.[2] Therefore, it is reasonable to assume that he would have said more, specifically more about Jesus, given the opportunity. Third, it is plain to see that Paul did in fact mention Jesus' name. This is precisely the point of contention in Paul's discussion with the Athenians (18-20). Fourth, those who maintain that Paul failed to mention the cross are interpreting too rigidly. While Luke does not explicitly mention Golgotha, it is clearly implied. After all, Paul's teaching on the resurrection (18, 31-32) makes no sense apart from the reality of Jesus' death. "Though the cross is missing in this

---

1. Carson, *Telling the Truth*, 391.
2. Carson, *The Gagging of God*, 503, n. 28.

summary report of his talk, the death of Christ must have been mentioned for him to mention the resurrection, and there is nothing to say that this was not clearly presented during his reasoning with the people of Athens prior to this event."[3]

All such attempts to treat this passage as something less than paradigmatic, or as bordering on an apostolic blunder, really miss the point of the address. Of course Jesus was mentioned, as Luke unambiguously records (18). Indeed, the tactics employed here closely parallel what Paul writes elsewhere, being consistent with his overall theology.

As to the notion that this mission failed, it is important to ask what standards we use to define success and failure. The real issue is not how many converts there were–this is always out of our control–but whether Paul faithfully communicated the truth to his audience. Of this there is no doubt. Evangelistic success is measured not by the number of positive responses to the gospel, which is ultimately God's business, but by how faithful we are to the gospel and to the whole counsel of God. We are to plant and water in various culturally sensitive ways, but God causes the growth (1 Corinthians 3:5-7).

Those who question the strategy here miss the wisdom this text provides, wisdom that must be extracted and applied. Paul communicates pertinent truths in culturally acceptable ways. Surely, this is not a sign of compromise but of brilliant contextualization. Far from making unnecessary concessions when among the Athenians, Paul provides, for all generations, the basic pattern to be followed when sharing the message of Jesus with those unacquainted with a Christian worldview.

---

3. Fernando, *Acts*, 477.

*"If God is at work,
perhaps we should embrace what he is doing."*

Pete Ward

"The postmodern pilgrim does not seek new truths, but seeks with new eyes eternal truths."

Leonard Sweet

In many ways our society has shifted from a modern to a postmodern outlook, and there are a variety of opinions as to the best way to engage our culture.

Those with modern inclinations continue to espouse traditional apologetics, while certain postmodern types have all but abandoned the need for apologetics.

But is it possible to forge ahead in another way? Can we incorporate some of the older arguments with some of the more helpful insights of postmodern thought?

If God is truly active in our world, it is imperative that we listen for His voice, allowing Him to teach us how to do postmodern apologetics.

Chapter Five

Apologetics in a Postmodern Era

Envisioning an Emergent Faith

Society is experiencing a monumental cultural shift as it moves from a modern to a postmodern paradigm. Today's priorities have changed, and the way we think has changed, as well. Dogmatism is out, and inclusion is in. Community has replaced individualism as a dominant theme. Certainty and confidence must compete with an increased skepticism and cynicism. Though these are surely generalizations, they reflect some of the current trends. In such a world, what role is there for Christian apologetics? Can (should) the faith be defended in a world that frowns upon anything too dogmatic? Indeed, if apologetics is to adapt to the times, what strategies are available?

Some within the church have continued to utilize modernistic approaches, believing that traditional arguments still have a place in a postmodern world. In fact postmodernism is seen by many as nothing but a threat to faith. Others, however, think that postmodern inclinations militate against the continuance of traditional apologetics; the discipline must either be abandoned or somehow adapted.[1]

---

1. Here, we will seek a balanced approach. On the one hand, there are certainly aspects of a modern apologetic that were either inappropriate or will have little impact in a postmodern world. On the other hand, there is no need to jettison the best features of modernity (or any other era). Since postmodern apologetics is the focus here, that will occupy most of the discussion. But the current setting in which we find ourselves must never become so narrow in focus as to exclude the wisdom of the past.

Given the changes that have taken place in popular culture, many Christians have taken a defensive stance, hoping to counter error and defend the truth against the onslaughts of religious pluralism and relativism. Indeed, there is little question that certain radical postmodern tendencies should be resisted. However, other trends may be conducive to the promulgation of the gospel in this era. As the church seeks to live faithfully within today's cultural milieu, it is imperative to honestly and creatively address the contemporary situation, giving "a reason for the hope that is in [us]" (1 Peter 3:15).

Apologetics, from the Greek word *apologia*, is often described as a reasoned defense of the faith. But this defensive approach must be supplemented by a more positive outlook in which the believability and attractiveness of the faith are highlighted. In our day this will include locating contemporary themes that are consistent with a Christian worldview and might be given expression in a postmodern world. Ultimately, however, it involves seeking the living God, who still guides those who have ears to hear.

The Postmodern Shift

During the modern era (1500-1960),[2] a number of pertinent ideas flourished, including a reliance on logic, a focus on the individual, an emphasis on the printed word, and an attitude of confidence regarding knowledge claims. All of these tendencies proved useful and yielded many benefits.

The problem with modernity, however, was that these features were often exaggerated to the point of imbalance. Logic was employed with such zeal and confidence that it fostered hubris, and other avenues of discovery (e.g., intuition) were discounted as issues of faith were approached in a more-or-less rationalistic fashion. Likewise, an excessive individualism led to a neglect of the corporate and a proneness to "do it yourself" spirituality.

As increased numbers came to recognize the abuses of the modern era, a new attitude began to emerge. Given that this was, at heart, a reaction against the prevailing tendencies of modernity, the cultural shift came to be known as *post*modern. Long describes postmodern-

---

2. Because it is difficul to identify the beginning and ending points of an era, there will always be a diffe ence of opinion about precise dates.

ism as a "moving away from reason by the autonomous self and moving toward relationship in community."[3] Smith adds that it includes such ideas as intuitiveness, skepticism, personal experience, and community.[4] Though defying simple explanation, postmodernism[5] can be understood as the pervasive cultural response to the trends of the modern era. In light of these changes, our task will be to consider what a postmodern *apologia* might look like.

A Postmodern Apologetic

A postmodern apologetic is one that takes seriously the challenges and questions that are relevant in today's cultural environment. Though we must be careful to guard against influences that might prove harmful, it is important to look with discerning eyes for indicators of God's presence in this era. What current ideas and cultural inclinations are evidences of His presence? Where has He left His "finger prints" on this world? These and related questions demand that we consider afresh the manner in which we do apologetics. We must begin, in other words, to envision a postmodern apologetic.

Postmodern Pause:
Avoiding Naivete When Encountering Popular Ideas

Before proceeding, however, it is important to mention a number of the potentially damaging influences of postmodern thought. Some

---

3. Jimmy Long, *Generating Hope: A Strategy for Reaching the Postmodern Generation* (Downers Grove, IL: InterVarsity Press, 1997), 61.

4. Chuck Smith, Jr., *The End of the World . . . As We Know It* (Colorado Springs, CO: Waterbrook Press, 2001), 46-47. See Smith's excellent discussion, 45-62.

5. Postmodernism has its proponents and its detractors. Philosophers, theologians, and others have differing opinions regarding this phenomenon. Though a good deal of this can be traced to the presuppositions of the individual, it is nonetheless true that postmodernism is an idea that is difficul to define. This, in turn, has led some to delineate diffe ent forms or types of postmodernism. Though somewhat simplistic, postmodernism can be separated into "soft" and "hard" versions. Hard postmodernism, which is the more radical type, is difficul to maintain from a Christian perspective. Soft postmodernism, on the other hand, is much more conducive to faith, providing a number of potentially beneficial a enues of thought.

of the more virulent forms of postmodernism reject anything like an all-encompassing universal standard in favor of local "truths"; what we are left with, in other words, is nothing but the opinions of individuals and communities.[6] Likewise, extreme versions of deconstructionism deny that words reflect, in any meaningful way, the actual state of affairs to which they supposedly point.[7] According to some, this renders impossible the discovery of anything (or Anyone) via written texts.[8] A related contention is that all truth claims are, at their core, effo ts to exert power and gain control. Whenever a person promulgates a belief system, his real intent is to get others to fall under his sway. The name of the game is p wer and control.[9]

6. The problem with this type of pluralism, however, is that in the desire to accept all avenues to God it actually detracts from the significance of the unique One described as "the way" (John 14:6).

7. See Stanley J. Grenz, *A Primer on Postmodernism* (Grand Rapids, MI: William B. Eerdmans Publishing Company, 1996), 148.

8. If, as some assert, no text (or spoken word) points to a reality beyond itself, if it is impossible to arrive at anything resembling objective reality, then radical postmoderns themselves are forced to allow their extreme views of deconstructionism to be deconstructed. Playing by their own rules, they must either admit the limitations of that which they proclaim with certainty (religious and philosophical pluralism, deconstructionism, etc.) or else allow for the possibility of objective truth claims. In other words, deconstructionists cannot actually live according to their own philosophy, since to do so would undermine the assumption that readers can actually understand their writings. Orthodox Christians, of course, affir that language *does* refer to something, that the Scriptures disclose truth, and that there is something (and Someone) behind the biblical texts. Indeed, believers have long declared that the biblical documents are intended to reveal their author.

9. In response to this contention, it would be foolish to deny the human tendency to seek mastery over others and to bolster one's position and reputation; Christians have often been guilty of this very thing. Still, this need not deter those whose quest is to see things the way they really are. Though no creature knows truth perfectly, it *is* possible, by God's enablement (Psalm 25:4-5, 8, 12), to know perfect truth adequately (John 8:31-32; 17:17). Furthermore, the fact remains that the allurement to power, though real and unavoidable, does not actually prohibit the acquisition of knowledge. Finally, it is important to recognize that the temptation to control is found among all human beings, including radical postmodernists. If their declarations are to be taken seriously, the books they write and the lectures they deliver are likewise effo ts to control. The i ony is remarkable.

In seeking to counter extreme claims, the church must neither succumb to relativism nor exaggerate its own grasp of the truth. On the one hand, Christian presuppositions affir that truth is accessible through general and special revelation; in other words, God can indeed speak, and we are able–by his providence, gifts, and grace, and because we are made in His image–to hear Him. On the other hand, it is essential to acknowledge the inherent limitations in all human knowing; though God has spoken, we are apt–due to human limitations (the fact that we are mere creatures) and divine transcendence (the fact that He is God)–to miss what He has said. The quest for knowledge must be tempered with humility, and boldness must be balanced by a recognition that the truths of which we speak are enveloped in great mystery.

In learning to deal with these issues, it is important not to over react or become condescending. Too many apologists have taken an overly critical stance toward postmoderns and, instead of attracting them to the faith, have actually driven them further away. Dulles, in describing certain groups, refers to this as an "overanxious defensiveness."[10] As believers and apologists, we must remind ourselves that our responsibility is not simply to be right but to "speak the truth in love" (Ephesians 4:15). Likewise, and just as important, we must remain open to the better postmodern themes, looking for God's imprint in our world.

Postmodern Positives
(Embracing What God is Doing Today)[11]

Many traditional thinkers have taken a stance against postmodernism, belittling its radical nature and encouraging others to do the

10. Avery Cardinal Dulles, *A History of Apologetics* (San Francisco, CA: Ignatius Press, 1999), 323.

11. A number of preliminary remarks are in order. (1) This is neither an effo t to criticize those not inclined to move in a postmodern direction nor a naive claim that moderns have never engaged in any of the effo ts mentioned below. The point is to recognize some positive ideas that have been brought to light in this era. (2) The e is no intent here to become so enamored with postmodernism that it becomes a theological version of political correctness. If moderns made some foolish decisions, postmoderns are just as liable to error. (3) The idea is not to leave behind the best features of modernity. It is never enough to give

same. Make no mistake about it; hard or radical postmodernism *is* an enemy of the truth, and its darker elements must be resisted. This does not mean, however, that every postmodern assertion is invalid or that one's relationship to it must be primarily adversarial.

In contrast to this mostly negative stance, there is much to garner from postmodernism, and those sensitive to contemporary concerns are better off than those who ignore the issues that have been given voice through the emerging church movement.[12] The beneficial features of postmodernism include an embrace of community as the context for faith, a recognition that God is not only knowable but also baffling, a ealization that the Lord himself (and not merely our ideas about him) must be encountered, an awareness of our place in the grand story God is telling, and a hopeful willingness to journey with others toward the truth. We will briefly examine these motifs.

---

mere lip service to the best ideas of previous generations. We must, rather, retain whatever is valid from any time, looking also to see what new things are available in our day. Though the emphasis here is on postmodern inclinations, a fully orbed apologetic will not fail to embrace modern ideas, as well. Indeed, some supposedly modern concepts, ideas that received much ink and were prominent during the modern era, are actually quite biblical in origin. To this degree we must approach postmodernism not as an end-all but as another aspect of our journey. (4) The key in all of these postmodern ideas is not simply to look or act postmodern, as helpful as that might be. The point, truly, is to locate God's activity in our age. What postmodernism does, in other words, is drive us back to our sacred texts wherein we discover that some of what is taking place around us is actually quite consistent with Scripture. Our goal is to hear God's voice as it echoes across time, listening for reverberations of His presence.

12. *Emergence* is a term often used to describe the new and sometimes unconventional realities that are emanating from people and groups that are postmodern in orientation. It basically depicts the unprecedented changes that are taking place in society in general and within segments of the church. For a brief discussion, see Dan Kimball, *The Emerging Church: Vintage Christianity for New Generations* (Grand Rapids, MI: Zondervan Publishing House, 2003), 13-17. McLaren adds this description: "We see God not as a potentate trying to keep serfs under control in the stasis of perpetual childhood, but rather as a parent inviting us to grow and mature, to become as good and beautiful and true as we can become–to emerge." Brian D. McLaren, *A Generous Orthodoxy* (Grand Rapids, MI: Zondervan Publishing House, 2004), 283.

Community Apologetics: Belonging as the Context for Faith

Though Christians have always given lip service to the notion of community, in practice they have sometimes been guilty of fostering an independent brand of faith. Following cultural inclinations, it is common to hear truth explained in terms of the individual, sanctification as something each person must do, and salvation itself as simply *my* response to the gospel.

By way of contrast, many in our day are captivated by community and driven by the friendships it facilitates. Though people have always needed to connect with one another, postmoderns are particularly concerned to find places of belonging. As a result, there is much talk about this theme.

This community orientation is something that is common in Scripture, finding its impetus in the fact that human beings are created in the image of a communing God.

> The fact that God is the social trinity–Father, Son, and Spirit–gives us some indication that the divine purpose for creation is directed toward the individual-in-relationship. Our gospel must address the human person within the context of the communities in which people are embedded.[13]

Just as, according to Christian theology, God is a plurality of persons, a divine community of interaction, so we are wired to commune. It is thus no surprise to find that most people desire to live their lives in conjunction with those who are like-minded.

Scripture is replete with examples of how this is might take place. For example when the early church was scattered due to persecution, there was a strong impetus to provide a haven for those who had lost everything. As Acts describes, "all those who had believed were together and had all things in common" (Acts 2:44). This is summarized by Paul, who instructs his readers to "Be devoted to one another in brotherly love" (Romans 12:10), which includes a willingness to "rejoice with those who rejoice and weep with those who weep" (Romans 12:15).

---

13. Grenz, *A Primer on Postmodernism*, 168-169.

Here, then, is a wonderful opportunity and privilege. We can be—individually and as faith communities—the place where love and truth coalesce. Indeed, 1 Peter 3:15, a key apologetics text, implicitly highlights this theme. The context of our *apologia*, the place where others might encounter God, is among those motivated to "give an answer for [their] hope" (1 Peter 3:15).

Hope, in other words, is observable. When we exude an expectation of better things, when purpose and truth emanate from our lives, we "set the stage" for the development of faith. Our responsibility involves much more than providing answers; it also entails an active demonstration of hope. A community of faith provides the framework, the subtle yet powerful effect, by which truth claims are given authentic expression. When truth so impacts believers, it fl ws outward and has a captivating influence.

Of course the manner in which this belonging motif takes shape will vary. But, whether through regular gatherings, casual activities, or by means of ongoing encounters and friendships with our neighbors, the point remains the same. Human beings need one another. All people crave places where they can feel free to be themselves and to explore life with those who actually care. A good part of a postmodern apologetic will entail providing those places.

When Christians are overly judgmental, when they remain aloof from society and only draw attention to what's wrong with it, when there does not seem to be even a hint of empathy for those who doubt, question, and hurt, the results are predictable. Postmoderns, more than their predecessors, are less willing to endure such attitudes.

Our challenge is to build relationships with others, learning to connect with them. These effo ts must never be manipulative or forced but rather expressions of a sincere concern for and enjoyment of our fellow-human beings. Our apologetic, in other words, must embrace the idea that belonging often precedes believing, and faith often develops best when it takes place within the framework of an already established bond. No matter how accurate our doctrinal beliefs or precise our theological formulations, it is imperative that we love and accept people in Jesus' name. In a postmodern world, a community of unconditional love is one of the strongest apologetics we can provide, for only within integrity-laced, loving relationships can we truly show that Jesus is Lord.[14]

Sacred Apologetics: Drawn to God through Mystery

Moderns tend to approach life in a rather dogmatic fashion, treating some of the more difficul questions of truth and life as if they are easily answerable. Part of this is understandable, for God has indeed revealed Himself to us. Given that God is truth (John 14:6), it makes sense that we would be confident about what He has shared with us.

That God reveals Himself is no surprise to Christians. On the other hand, believers have not always been willing to admit, or even be cognizant of the fact, that many things about God are not so easily deciphered. Though He has revealed many things, "the secret things" are hidden from our view. The Lord both reveals *and* conceals (see Deuteronomy 29:29).

Postmoderns, some who have grown skeptical of overly confident claims, tend to reject anything that sounds too dogmatic, (sometimes to the point of embracing outright skepticism), preferring a humbler approach to knowledge. This does not mean that postmoderns themselves are necessarily more humble than their predecessors. It does mean, however, that their general philosophy of life is one in which close mindedness and unnecessarily narrow views are despised.[15]

Fortunately, this dovetails nicely into a Christian worldview. Scripture not only provides parameters for living and truths for

---

14. What is community? Our apologetic must entail far more than "join us at church." What's more, we must not be so naive as to think that we can manufacture some sort of artificial place of belonging. More relevant would be a concerted effo t to simply love our neighbors–not love as a means of coercing a decision, not love in order to get others to join our congregations, not love as a tool of religious manipulation, but simply love in the name of Jesus. A postmodern apologetic is one that provides an environment where the people we encounter can feel comfortable (or, when appropriate, convicted), accepted, and (hopefully) willing to journey with us.

15. Of course dogmatic skeptics are sometimes the most close-minded of all, refusing to apply their own principles of skepticism to the views they proclaim. All humans are prone to hubris.

believing, but it also declares that many things defy the creature's understanding. One avenue by which we can approach matters of faith, therefore, is to recognize, even embrace, the reality of human ignorance in the presence of God. A Christian apologetic is fortified by the idea that we can only grasp deity in part, that the Lord will always exceed our effo ts to comprehensively understand Him.

A part of our apologetic strategy, if it is to be simultaneously postmodern and (more importantly) Christian, will be to place life's mysteries within the broader context of an often mysterious God.[16] This mystery template enables us to consider the difficul questions we encounter in an unpretentious fashion. Likewise, to the degree that we display spiritual and intellectual modesty, it affo ds us the opportunity to speak with more boldness about those matters which are *not* hidden from sight.

Can we not revel in the fact that many things about our Creator are far beyond us? Would it not be conducive to building relationships for us to admit that there are often times when we, too, "don't get it"? Indeed, would it not be refreshing for us to exhibit an attitude of combined humility and confidence? Yes, we know some things because God has revealed them to us; these must be humbly and appropriately shared. But, other things exceed our understanding, and even the things we truly know about God are enveloped in deep mystery. Such is the case when dealing with the great "I am." As Paul once wrote: "We know in part" (1 Corinthians 13). Isaiah puts it this way: "But to this one I will look, to him who is humble and contrite of spirit, and who trembles at My word" (66:2). A postmodern apologetic is one that invites others into the presence of the knowable but also mysterious deity.

Existential Apologetics: Facilitating Connectivity

During the modern era, the temptation was to spend an inordinate amount of time and energy constructing theories, sometimes mistak-

---

16. Rudolf Otto popularized the idea of the *mysterium tremendum*, the awful mystery. The basic idea is that God can be encountered in ways that transcended (not contradict) the rational. See Rudolf Otto, *The Idea of the Holy* (New York: Oxford University Press, 1958).

ing meaning for application and confusing knowledge about God with an actual acquaintance with Him. Clearly, both of these are needed if we are going to live in accordance with the Bible. That is, there is a relationship between the ideas we hold *about* God and the relationship we have *with* Him. Still, with the church's determination to remain doctrinally sound and theologically informed, the personal matter of connecting with God was sometimes minimized.[17]

In contrast, postmoderns have a deep sense of wanting to encounter the truth and not merely formulate theories about it. The e is, as might be expected, a tendency to go too far in the other direction and to neglect theory in favor of what "feels good." Still, the postmodern desire to encounter the transcendent is a potentially healthy impulse.

In many places the Bible assumes this personal encounter with the truth. Paul, for instance, makes clear his passion for God, describing it in terms of "knowing Him" (Philippians 3:10). Likewise, Peter speaks of growing "in the grace and knowledge of our Lord and Savior" (2 Peter 3:18), and John writes of possessing life *through the Son* (1 John 5:11-12 - "having the Son" is the way he puts it). In all of these passages, *descriptive knowledge of God* intersects with *a personal encounter with God*. Our effo ts, therefore, must be directed not only toward providing accurate information but actually pointing others to the One who is "not far from each one of us" (Acts 17:27).

Concerning a Christian apologetic, this theme reminds us that, while intellectual matters are certainly relevant, the goal of it all is to be united with one's Maker. Informing others of the Maker's identity is still necessary, of course, but we must not neglect to see that it is possible to connect with God despite our imperfect knowledge of Him. Apologists must not assume that people must first accept various intellectual arguments before they can actually access God. While we can provide motivation for faith and content for making informed faith decisions, it is always true–however accurate or inaccurate our communication–that God Himself is ever-present. Knowing of the gracious Lord's continual presence enables us to avoid the error of making apologetics more of an obstacle to faith than a facilitator of it. Hence, a part of our apologetic strategy will

---

17. One obvious exception to this trend is found among Pentecostal and Charismatic believers who have always emphasized the relational.

be to encourage and provide reasons for people to look outside of themselves. Whether or not we convince them on this or that point, it is nonetheless possible they may contact (or be contacted by!) the One we are attempting to describe. Our apologetic must include an effo t to promote real-life encounters with God.

Narrative Apologetics: Participating in the Story

One key feature of postmodern thought is its fascination with narrative. While moderns were drawn to propositions, postmoderns are attracted to stories. From the vantage point of the Bible, this is very significant, for a good portion of Scripture takes this form. From the story of the nation of Israel to the accounts of the early church, the narrative sections of Scripture play a vital role. Indeed, Jesus' ministry was often driven by this story-telling agenda as He shared parables with the people of His day (Matthew 22:1ff; ark 4:1ff).

It is with good reason, therefore, that the church learns to re-emphasize this narrative approach. Rather than treating the stories of Scripture as pointers to abstract propositions, as mere addendums to biblical doctrines, the stories themselves become essential features of the church's mission.

Of course the postmodern penchant for story does not, in itself, guarantee any type of spiritual benefit. It does, however, provide ample reason for believing that human beings are "wired" for story.

> The business of the church is to tell and to embody a story, the story of God's mighty acts in creation and redemption and of God's promises concerning what will be in the end. The church affirm the truth of this story by celebrating it, interpreting it, and enacting it in the life of the contemporary world.[18]

Regarding apologetics, there are hints in Scripture that might assist us along the way. One of these would be a recounting of those stories in which God's people encountered various circumstances, including those that involved persecution and suffering. For instance, as

---

18. Lesslie Newbigin, *Proper Confidence: Faith, Doubt and Certainty in Christian Discipleship* (Grand Rapids, MI: William B. Eerdmans Publishing Company, 1995), 76.

one contemplates the story of Joseph's mistreatment, it is easy to recognize both the degree of suffering he endured and the amazing way he handled hard times (Genesis 50:20). Of course the most compelling story is that of Jesus. His relationships with the disciples, His confrontation with the religious establishment of His day, His "outside the box" brand of spirituality–all of these are truly captivating. Our apologetic must embrace these stories, allowing their power to impact the lives of others.

In keeping with this story-telling paradigm, it is also important to allow our apologetic to fl w from the stories that comprise our lives. We all have tales to tell, disappointments to recount, triumphs to repeat, doubts to acknowledge, hope to proclaim. Moderns were good at stating propositions (e.g., Jesus is Lord) and defending facts (e.g., He rose from the grave). Without ignoring any of these, we must invite others into our personal space where they can observe what this death-defying Savior does in the lives of real people. We must be careful, of course, not to fabricate stories, exaggerate our experiences, make ourselves the hero of every situation, or offer more than God Himself has promised. Inauthentic claims are never an option in this or any other era. But, and this is crucial, we must be able to share real stories, both our own and those within Scripture, affo ding men and women the opportunity to consider the story that God may already be telling in their lives.

Teleological Apologetics: Journeying Toward the Truth[19]

Some within the church place an emphasis on what might be termed immediate transformation. A crisis experience or a decision is held

---

19. Teleological apologetics is mentioned both here and in Chapter 4. Both instances deal with apologetics as directional and personal. That is, they prompt a journey (the direction) to Jesus (the person). In Chapter 4 the goal of apologetics is in view, that is, leading people to the *telos*, Jesus. This implies a process but highlights the goal. In Chapter 5 the process is in view, that is, the gradual nature of spiritual growth and maturity. This implies the goal but highlights the step-by-step response to the gospel. Emphasizing diffe ent characteristics of a teleological approach, together they convey the notion that apologetics must include a personal, process-oriented component. In essence this involves calling people to follow Jesus.

out as the pathway to imminent blessing. If we have needs, a "power encounter" can occur in which the Holy Spirit alters hearts, changes perspectives, and enables people to see their own lives from a different perspective.

No one who wants to be faithful to Scripture can deny the possibility of such encounters. Certainly, God can intervene in our lives in such a way as to radically change us. This "here and now" approach is not to be despised, for none of us can predict how God will work to reach and enliven His followers. The e is little doubt, in other words, that the ever-present Lord can and does provide direct and sometimes spontaneous aid.

On the other hand, some traditional Christians have taken this instant transformation model too far, treating spirituality as primarily a series of encounters and neglecting to see that it is also a journey. Postmoderns resonate with this gradual approach, recognizing that life, including one's spiritual life, usually entails a process. Paul sounds this theme when he describes the life of faith as something to be "worked out" over time (Philippians 2:12ff). Likewise, Peter speaks of ongoing diligence and growth as the pattern for Jesus' disciples (2 Peter 3:14-18).

When considering a postmodern apologetic, it is important to look to God expectantly for immediate assistance but to realize, as well, that many matters are worked out over the course of a lifetime. While God can indeed change us in an instant, it is more often the case that He works in our hearts and lives to transform us step-by-step. As to our apologetic, it is imperative that we treat our relationships with others not so much as effo ts to win them over immediately but as a part of a larger, ongoing story.

Many of us can testify to the fact that we've changed (hopefully for the better) over time. Sometimes practically, sometimes theologically, we mature. If this is true of us, should we not affo d others the time and space to make gradual changes in their own lives? Some traditional apologists drive people away by insisting that the truths they espouse should be accepted without delay. The irony of this is that some of these same apologists took many years before they embraced the faith. Perhaps a better approach would be that which is hinted at in Romans. The e, Paul said, "I planted the seed, Apollos watered it, but God made it grow" (1 Corinthians 3:6). The e is patience built into this kind of thinking. Jesus was the consummate example of this outlook, for He walked and talked with His followers, living and teaching among them regularly. Though He often challenged them, and while He never hesitated to call them to repentance, He never coerced them in such a way as to violate their humanity. Over time, Jesus encouraged others to come to grips with His purpose and mission, even enduring their foolish choices. Along the way, He provided correction and kindness, but He seemed content to allow the cumulative impact of His words and life to gradually lead them in the right direction. A postmodern apologetic must further this journeying approach.

Conclusion

The subjects addressed here are a mere sampling of themes that contribute to a postmodern perspective on apologetics. As God is sovereign in every era, and due to the fact that He has seen fit to direct us in this postmodern way, it is incumbent upon believers to pay attention to what He might be teaching us today. With a healthy openness to what God is doing in our world, combined with a commitment to the "once for all" nature of the Christian faith, it is possible to benefit from current societal inclinations.

In order to cultivate a postmodern apologetic, certain relevant motifs will have to be taken seriously, some of which have been surveyed here. But if we are going to adapt and keep pace with the times, we must insist that apologetics take place within the arena of everyday life. We can no longer remain at the distance, observing and then critiquing societal tendencies, seeking merely to protect the faithful from the errors that abound. Though avoiding naivete, we must learn, as well, to genuinely connect with people, not as know-it-all experts but as fellow travelers who long to share the love of Jesus with others. An authentic, timely, Spirit-led apologetic demands nothing less.

"What we are doing is pointing people toward God and encouraging them to interact with his Spirit."

Ron Martoia

"All truths are easy to understand once they are discovered; the point is to discover them."

Galileo

Sometimes we lose track of what really matters. Theories and ideas, true as they might be, can distract us from what's taking place all around us.

It is important, therefore, to pay attention to real-life situations and to keep our eyes open to the manner in which God changes men and women.

While pure pragmatism is insufficient—after all, it is possible to "help" others in ways that violate other principles and produce harm—it is important to observe what avenues God uses to bless people. Here we will briefly investigate some of these.

Chapter Six

Truth Tactics

Miscellaneous Thoughts on Apologetics

When it comes to sharing the gospel, a wide variety of factors influence any person's receptivity to the message. The discipline of apologetics is concerned to address these factors, hoping to clear a way for people to embrace the good news.[1]

But if we are going to be successful communicators of the truth, we must be contemplative and creative about this truth-telling endeavor. Apologetics, in other words, must expand beyond merely providing answers (important as this can be), wisely and imaginatively addressing broader realities.

Along these lines, Kelly James Clark provides a number of methodological recommendations, noting that Christian apologists can benefi from a recognition of components that influence belief. Clark notes,

> the scales can fall from the mind's eye in a wide variety of means: on a mountain top, while listening to a sermon, through a humbling experience, or by reading *The Chronicles of Narnia*. . . . I believe we need to pay a lot more attention to how actual people acquire beliefs.[2]

---

1. This task is defined in one place as "the defense and confirmation of the gospel" (Philippians 1:7; 16). Another passage, following the same theme, urges believers to "make a defense" of their hope (1 Peter 3:15).

2. Steven B. Cowan, ed., *Five Views of Apologetics*, The Counterpoint Series, (Grand Rapids, MI: Zondervan Publishing House, 2000), 273.

It is of course important to guard against confusing mere sentimentality with actual conversion. Authenticity, not communicative trickery, must be the guiding force in our effo ts. That said, there may be a number of elements (emotional, cognitive, psychological, cultural) that contribute to a genuine application of the truth and play a role in developing a helpful apologetic.

The strategies delineated here will be of a general sort, drawing attention to a number of ideas that are relevant to successful apologetics. Some of these are geared toward our contemporary situation. Many of them are reflecti e of timeless concepts. Each of them is intended to properly influence our app oach to apologetics.

1. *The form and style of the worshiping community can facilitate apologetics.*

When discussing the truth with non-Christians, it is desirable to have them eventually connect with other believers, spending time (formally and informally) among those who seek to follow Jesus. To this end it is certainly discouraging that some within the church, having isolated themselves from (real or imagined) societal influences, are ill-equipped to meet people where they are. Put bluntly, the atmosphere of certain Christian groups is something less than appealing.

This is not to say that the church ought to have as its first priority a desire to entertain the world.[3] Nor should believers be found frantically attempting to mimic secular culture. The e is certainly no need to abandon ecclesiastic traditions simply in order to appease those driven by a politically correct agenda. The e is a need, however, to have relevant (and not merely shallow) relationships with the people we meet. Indeed, there is much to be gained from genuine (and not hypercritical) encounters with one's culture.

---

3. Entertainment has often been criticized by those who deem it inappropriate to connect with spirituality, and the point is well taken. After all, it is wrong to compromise content in order to simply pacify an audience. Some churches have done just that, allowing hype to take precedence over substance. However, the notion of entertainment can also refer to cordially receiving others, capturing and maintaining their interest. While entertainment has often been rightly criticized, there are times when a more compelling style is precisely what we need.

If the church is to be effecti e, it must appeal to postmodern people, cultivating an atmosphere that is safe, enjoyable, and authentic. A good measure of the church's future success is contingent, humanly speaking, on its ability to embody a winsome spirituality. Drawing on the resources of the larger Christian community, believers must create a climate in which apologetics can flourish.

2. *Sometimes, it is just as important to show that Christianity is embraced by intellectuals, as it is to demonstrate specific intellectual arguments.*

   Not every person is concerned about detailed apologetic arguments. Some are looking for something much simpler. They are not so much interested in carefully analyzing the evidence as they are in the fact that there is evidence in the first place. A well-organized defense of the faith is not their goal; they are merely concerned that such a defense exists.

   As a parallel, one might consider the subject of national security. The e is much that goes into protecting a country, and some people are quite intrigued by the actual hardware that is utilized to that end, the planes and tanks and number of soldiers. But many others are not. For them, the details do not much matter. What they are looking for is a general assurance that their country is safe.

   The same can be true when doing apologetics. It is important not to lose people amid a myriad of arguments that they may not be particularly interested in. For many individuals the cosmological argument is too deep, and philosophical discussions are not impressive. It is enough that Christians are able to simply point out that there are indeed scientists, philosophers, and other intellectuals who accept a theistic/Christian worldview as true.

3. *Conversion is a call to a "higher" life, transforming a person's perspective and priorities, but it is still a human life, resembling, in many ways, the life of the past.*

   Some people have funny ideas about what it means to become a Christian, thinking that it involves a complete rejection of nearly everything to which a person is accustomed. Certain fundamentalist groups foster this idea by maintaining rigid standards, often unspoken, which severely (and unfairly) limit the freedom of those who want to follow Jesus. These can relate to many areas, from length of hair and style of clothing to brand of music and general attitude. Sometimes these extra-biblical regulations are explicitly stated, while in certain cases the "rules" are part of a subtle legalistic attitude.

What is unavoidable and quite sobering is the thought that non-Christians naturally assume they are being urged to take on the characteristics of those who are sharing the truth with them. How sad, then, when believers portray faith in a rather odd fashion. In contrast how refreshing it is to find a believer who knows (and clarifies) the diffe ence between divine revelation (what God has said) and human tradition (what we say). To become a Christian is to reject harmful things and embody love; these are a large part of what it's all about. But weirdness simply must be avoided.[4]

Conversion entails a radical break with the world. Rebellion is to be rejected and idols disowned (1 Thessalonians 1:9; 1 John 5:21). Indeed, even otherwise harmless things must not be allowed to take the priority they once did (see Matthew 13:22; Mark 4:18-10; Luke 8:14). The call to follow Jesus, in other words, involves change.

At the same time, there are numerous ways in which a convert remains unaltered. Believers still have hobbies, enjoy sports, and look forward to vacation. They feel, laugh, and cry. Often they are tempted, and sometimes they doubt.

While it is true that repentance leads to a fundamental spiritual reorientation (2 Corinthians 5:17), many things remain outwardly (and sometimes inwardly) the same. Of course inher-

---

4. The e is a sense, of course, in which the behavior of godly people will appear odd to outsiders. When you pursue holiness, honesty, and integrity, those repulsed by such virtues often find it difficul to accept them as "normal." These virtues, however, are not actually bizarre but are misidentified or mislabeled by those who operate from a skewed perspective. Some behavior is truly strange, while other behavior is only perceived to be so.

ently evil matters are to be turned from, and the overemphasis of innocent things must be guarded against. But a large part of the faith entails not so much external alterations but a new outlook, seeing the world through diffe ent "lenses." Work, family life, leisure activities, and a whole host of other categories are elevated to a higher plane; everything takes on greater relevance.

As far as apologetic strategy is concerned, it is important to correct the wrong perceptions many have about Christianity. Our message is one of change and renewal, but it is not a rejection of one's personality. Quite the contrary. Our true selves begin to flourish as e embrace God's purpose.

4. *To become a follower of Jesus involves the recognition of the cost of discipleship, as well as the anticipation of a joyful new life.*

Following God in this world is a challenge, and every would-be disciple must "take up his cross daily" (Luke 9:23). Since the believer is marked by diffe ent priorities than many non-Christians, an inevitable friction will occur between the two parties. Jesus was up front about this: "A slave is not greater than his master. If they persecuted Me, they will also persecute you" (John 15:20). Paul said the same thing, emphasizing that the pursuit of godliness inevitably leads to some measure of difficult (2 Timothy 3:12). Believers pursue a life that includes self-forgetfulness (living for God and others), potential misunderstanding (from those outside–and sometimes inside–the believing community), and inevitable opposition (from those who suppress and decry the ways of God in the world). Following Jesus, in other words, is a serious matter, and apologists must, when appropriate, communicate this fact.

On the other hand, the life of a believer is certainly much more than struggle, for through Jesus we connect with our Maker and receive tremendous spiritual benefits (Ezekiel 11:19; Colossians 1:12-14). Having access to the ever-present God, life takes on a grander purpose (Hebrews 6:17-20), and hope takes root in our lives (1 Thessalonians 5:13- 18). As the Psalmist declares, "Taste and see that the Lord is good" (Psalm 34:8). Or, in the words of Jesus: "I came that they may have life, and have it abundantly" (John 10:10).

As apologists and communicators of the gospel, it is essential that we allow these two elements to inform our perspective and the message we share with others. To mention only the blessings of faith is to neglect the hard realities of living in a fallen world; potentially, this could lead to a misrepresentation of Jesus' role in our lives. At the very least, it might cause the uninformed believer, the believer who expects only happy experiences, to despair when confronted by hard times. On the other hand, to highlight only the difficultie and duties of the Christian life is to neglect the beauty and peace associated with faith; this, too, leads to discouragement.

Followers of Jesus are expected to persevere amid adversity that cannot be completely avoided. Likewise, they are encouraged to bask in the infinite wonder of a union with God. A rightly balanced approach to apologetics must communicate both facets of kingdom life.

5. *Apologists must exude and promote hope.*[5]

In 1 Peter 3:15, Peter urges his readers to "give an account for the hope that is in [them]." While many apologists rightly emphasize the need to provide support for Christian hope, not as many elaborate on hope itself. What Peter is saying is that the believer's hope ought to be so obvious that outsiders feel compelled to inquire about the nature of such certitude and excitement.

In the ancient world, there were many reasons to be discouraged. Persecution, and even martyrdom, was common, and life was not easy. It is with good reason, then, that hope played such a critical role in the life of the church. Though perilous times may come, a wonderful future is promised through Jesus (1 Thessalonians 4:13-5:11; 1 ohn 3:1-3).

Believers today are also beset by various trials. Though the extent of persecution in the West nowhere approaches that which is encountered by Christians in foreign lands, all believers have

---

5. See Chapter 1, Hope's Reason, for more commentary on this topic.

experienced heartache of one sort or another. With all the sadness that abounds, it is important to have a sure hope, to possess something that lasts. This is precisely what the gospel proclaims. Th ough the redemptive labors of God's Son, there is forgiveness and joy now, but the best is yet to come.

What do people in a fallen world long for? Among other factors, they desire stability and assurance. Christianity explains where these are found, providing hope for a better tomorrow.[6] It is thus legitimate to draw attention not merely to a catalogue of general evidences for faith but to the fact that these give weight to what faith is all about, a transformed future and a present that is informed and motivated by such promises. Hope, in other words, is a powerful attention getter, drawing people to hope's true Source.

6. *In communicating with others, it is important to balance evidence and mystery, certainty and ignorance.*

Christianity is not merely one of a number of legitimate belief systems, which is why believers have long maintained that the historic faith is unique.[7] Nothing explains life as the Christian Scriptures do, and nothing transforms lives more profoundly than an encounter with the living God.

---

6. The e is an obvious eschatological focus to this hope; that is, hope finds its complete fulfillment at the end of this present age. In biblical usage, however, there is also a sense in which the eschaton, i.e., the age to come, overlaps and infiltrates the present. God's Spirit allows those with faith to experience some measure of the future even now; this is sometimes referred to as "the now and the not yet." Far from producing an unrealistic "pie-in-the-sky" attitude, faith in the future is intended to have an impact and a hope-inducing effect on the here-and-now.

7. One might of course ask what constitutes "unique," especially given our human propensity to misinterpret and the long history of divisions within the household of faith. First, it is important to acknowledge that we *have* often made errors and misguided judgments. Second, even misguided errors are consistent with the broad worldview that, diffe ences admitted, can be located with remarkable consistency throughout church history. Thi d, the point in declaring a Christian worldview is not that we should close ourselves off from new insights; rather, it is to locate the sphere were worldview formulation takes place, namely within the church, connected to historic faith, centered in Scripture, and dependent upon God.

What's more, believers maintain that "the faith which was once for all handed down to the saints" (Jude 1:3) provides the best and fullest explanation for matters that most puzzle human beings. Subjects like the problem of human suffering are most helpfully understood from the perspective of Christian truth claims.

However, as many have discovered, not every objection to theism in general and Christianity in particular is easy to handle. Indeed, effectively communicating the truth with others can be a complicated and challenging endeavor. Though we are not left in the dark, many things remain puzzling, and certain objections to faith can only be answered tentatively.[8] This is why, for example, Reformed Epistemological apologists have often pointed out that we should be humble in our presentation of arguments.[9] Some things, frankly, defy explanation.

It is at this point that we must avoid extremes. While some cower in fear when questioned about their faith, thinking that answers are unavailable, others are so arrogant as to assume that their formulation of the faith easily satisfies every person. But neither of these approaches is appropriate.

A better way ahead is to balance optimism and ignorance. Since God has communicated His will, we have every reason to proclaim it. At the same time, there is no reason to arrogantly assert that we have answers that are not yet (fully) available. We know certain things, and these ought to be made clear. But many things are beyond our current ability to comprehend.

---

8. Consider, for instance, the problem of evil. While Scripture provides plausible and hope-filled explanations for pain and suffering, certain situations are very difficul to grasp. Why does God sometimes allow evil to dominate the lives of His children? Why do little babies die? And, in all of this, how can a sovereign God remain free from blame in events He ultimately controls? While the Bible is not silent on these issues, not every answer is provided.

9. *Five Views*, 282-283. Also, see Kelly James Clark, *When Faith Is Not Enough* (Grand Rapids, MI: William B. Eerdmans Publishing Company, 1997), passim.

Of course none of this should surprise us, for we are called to embrace the true God, a being who can be described and understood but whose ways are also far above us. This, it seems, is what Scripture requires, and it is what many people appreciate. It is proper, therefore, even desirable, to be both confident and humble when it comes to matters of faith and apologetics.

7. *The unique features of the faith should be highlighted.*

Many people believe that all religions are essentially the same. They are but diffe ent avenues leading to the same God. It is not so important what religion one chooses; it only matters that some path is taken.

But is such a perspective plausible? After all, how can viewpoints that are in many ways antithetical be treated as parallel? While there are similarities between certain religious philosophies, there are also dissimilarities. It may be convenient to believe in some type of religious pluralism, but it is hardly makes sense of all of the facts.[10]

If God exists, and if He has revealed Himself, at least some of His ways would likely be discernible. Among a plethora of religious ideas, the true God would stand out from the crowd. In keeping with this assumption, the Christian faith makes unique truth claims.

The prime example, of course, is Jesus. As the God-man, no other figu e in human history bridges the gap separating humanity from its Creator (1 Timothy 2:5). No one else made such claims to deity and then backed them up with miraculous demonstrations of power (Mark 2:1-12; John 8:53-9:41). No other person is so like us (Hebrews 2:17-18; 4:15) and yet so dissimilar (Mark 2:1-12; 4:35-41). Truly, He is one of a kind (John 3:16).[11]

---

10. For an analysis of and a Christian response to pluralism, see D. A. Carson, *The Gagging of God: Christianity Confronts Pluralism* (Grand Rapids, MI: Zondervan Publishing House, 1996).

11. The Greek term from John 3:16 that is often translated "only begotten" is *monogeneis*, which means something like "one of a kind."

Next, there is the fact that Christianity alone, among the world religions, provides access to God for free.[12] Because of what Jesus has accomplished, men and women need not attempt to earn God's favor. All that is required is simple faith, a childlike reliance on God's Son to provide a right standing before the bar of heaven (Romans 3:21-28; Galatians 3:26; Philippians 3:8-9; 1 John 5:9-13).

While there are certain parallels between Christianity and other world religions, there are also many differences. The similarities, where they are truly present, provide points of contact between adherents to different traditions. The differences, on the other hand, are what make Jesus special. One task of apologetics is to highlight the unparalleled features of the faith.[13]

8. *There is a cultural benefit to be gained from engaging secular society with a sound apologetic.*

One factor that is sometimes missed in an apologetic encounter is the broader influence it can have on a culture. There is a type of residual effect in any intelligent presentation of the truth. "Even if few are converted through apologetic arguments, still such arguments help to shape an intellectual milieu in which the gospel can still be heard as a credible alternative."[14] This is especially the case when an apologist reaches a wider audience.

By means of a television interview, a debate, a well-written letter to a local newspaper, and many other avenues, a subtle message is sent to those who encounter the truth. Indeed, it is difficult to measure the positive interrelational impact of those

---

12. Of course many will simply assume some sort of universalism. With such individuals, it will be necessary to convey an accurate view of God and humanity. To the degree that one places the true God alongside of fallen human beings, some sense of human culpability and divine justice becomes evident. While universalistic thought is both popular and convenient, it does not match reality. When necessary, apologists need to clarify these matters.

13. Drawing attention to faith's unique features does not automatically require a combative posture. Though there are times when a clear contrast must be made between authentic and counterfeit claims, often the mere demonstration of "the way, and the truth, and the life" is enough to indicate the distinction between truth and falsehood.

14. *Five Views*, 288-289.

who humbly live out their faith. As a result, the way of Jesus is seen as plausible and appealing.

Perhaps, over time, a number of people will be more open to the faith because of the reputation built through the effo ts of thoughtful and caring communicators.

9. *It is important for apologists to consider the needs of non-readers.*

The best teachers are also learners, and this learning is facilitated through a variety of resources. Yet, however one comes to grow in the knowledge of God, it would be difficul to overstate the value of the written medium. It is often through literature that we are exposed to ideas, both abstract and practical, that shape our hearts and lives.

Due to this emphasis, many Christians utilize the printed word in an effo t to communicate the gospel. But what should we do when seeking to influence those who seldom or never read? It is this very question that numerous apologists have ignored. Some would rather ridicule the illiteracy of individuals than seek ways of reaching them. For others, the preferred method involves coercing non-readers, "force feeding" them literature.

While there is surely a place for encouraging people to read, it will also be important to reach out to those who are not likely to pick up a book or pamphlet. Michael Green offers this analysis:

> I am not aware that anyone has really mastered the art of effecti e and life-changing communication of the gospel with people who rarely read. But it is absolutely vital that we try. After all, the first Christians were for the most part illiterate. In many parts of the world today in which the gospel is spreading fast, people cannot read.[15]

Green suggests, among other things, that apologists can benefit from story-telling, visual aids, and the sharing of life experi-

---

15. Michael Green and Alister McGrath, *How Shall We Reach Them? Defending and Communicating the Christian Faith to Nonbelievers* (Nashville, TN: Thomas elson Publishers, 1995), 217

ences. These and other strategies will have to be employed if believers expect to have any real impact among those who are not literature driven.

10. *It is important to learn the art of indirect apologetics.*

A quick survey of the New Testament reveals that there are many ways to communicate the gospel. Sometimes the best approach is direct, simply telling people what they must do to be right with God. Peter's Pentecost sermon is one such example (Acts 2:14-40), as are Jesus' dealings with certain individuals (John 12:44-50). A direct approach entails a straightforward announcement that people must turn from their (faulty) ways, believe (the truth), and follow Jesus.

But in some situations, the best plan is more gradual and indirect. Think, for instance, of Paul's ministry in Athens (Acts 17:22-31). Paul did not bombard the Athenians with truths they could never have assimilated. Instead, he began in their world and led them gradually toward Christ. Jesus often used this same strategy. By asking questions, telling stories, and simply rubbing shoulders with His contemporaries, He was content to share general ideas with them (e.g., Mark 4:1-34; 7:1-23; 10:13-31, 46-52; 12:1-44). These ideas were certainly the outworking of a biblical worldview, but Jesus usually refrained from proclaiming Himself in a direct fashion. The indirect approach involves meeting people where they are, seeking common-ground, and applying the truth in an incremental fashion.

It is imperative for apologists to think not only in terms of direct proclamation (though this is certainly needed) but also in terms of indirect communication. The e are many facets of life that can be dealt with in a Christian way, without stuffin the gospel down people's throats. Some are not ripe for hearing the message of God's Son. But this does not mean they are unreceptive to everything that fl ws from a Christian perspective.

Interestingly, the world has long used this indirect method. While there have been numerous frontal assaults on the kingdom of God, it is often the subtle influences that have the most powerful impact. When a television sitcom merely assumes that premarital or extramarital relations are normal, no one makes much of a fuss. Yet, over the long haul, many observers are indeed influenced by what they watch. Suddenly, sexual activity outside of marriage does not seem like such a bad thing. This is further complicated when the television characters, those involved in these inappropriate relationships, are portrayed as otherwise nice people. What happens here is that an indirect message is provided, and those who "hear" it are led, step by step, to simply accept the message as true.

We can utilize indirect communication, as well. In the realm of politics, Scriptural values can be implemented. When it comes to life's hardships, a godly attitude might catch the attention of onlookers. Various kinds of relationships can be governed by proper beliefs. Homemakers, teachers, factory workers, and countless others can conduct their lives (morally, intellectually, and verbally) in such a way that those who are watching cannot help but see the truth. Then, when a direct word about Jesus is spoken, it might not appear foreign or disingenuous.

The intention here is not to avoid direct methods when they are appropriate. The goal, rather, is to show that the gospel can be communicated in a multiplicity of ways, some which are indirect. Jesus told His disciples they ought to be as "shrewd as serpents and as harmless as doves" (Matthew 10:16). This surely clears the way for indirect apologetics.

Conclusion

Believers are privileged to be emissaries of the living God, heralds of hope, and envoys of divinely revealed truths. It is therefore imperative that we approach apologetics with our eyes open. This includes an awareness and implementation of important ideas, some of which have been delineated here. With hearts and minds in gear, we will be better equipped to share the message that matters most with those who long for meaning and hope. To this end we must utilize all legitimate tactics, sharing the truth and love of Jesus with faith and humility.

"Once we take our eyes away from ourselves, from our interests, from our own rights, privileges, ambitions; then they will become clear to see Jesus around us."

Mother Teresa

"Love is, above all, the gift of oneself."

Jean Anouilh

In 1 Corinthians 13:13, Paul highlights the famous triad: faith, hope, and love. At the end of the day, these are the things that matter most. Faith creates hope and informs love. Hope motivates faith and sustains love. And love authenticates faith even as it confirms the legitimacy of hope. Of these three, however, one is primary: love.

If love is that important, it ought to play a role in everything we do, including apologetics. Whatever evidence we produce, however convincing our arguments or airtight our reasoning, we accomplish nothing without love.

The God who is love, and who has demonstrated love, calls us to a life of love. The only truly complete apologia, therefore, is one that is inextricably linked to "the greatest of these." Love, then, is the ultimate apologetic.

Chapter Seven

The Ultimate Apologetic[1]

Love and Human Relationships

> "Let your light shine before men in such a way that they may see your good works, and glorify your Father who is in heaven" (Matthew 5:16).

These words capture the essence of what truly matters when it comes to our relationships with others. Presenting evidence for the Christian faith or seeking to demonstrate the reasonableness of a theistic worldview, significant as these are, pale in comparison to our ability, as Jesus puts it, to shine. It is in this way that we display righteous and godly living, for such shining draws attention to God. The God who is invisible to human eyes is made visible through the works of His followers.

A closer look at the immediate context of Matthew 5 makes this even more clear. For instance in verse 13, believers are described as "the salt of the earth" and in verses 14 and 15 as "the light of the world." We are to live in such a way that we add flavor to society, preventing moral and spiritual decay, and we are to illuminate the ways of God for others. While the manner in which we give expression to these realities may not always be clear, what *is* clear is that "People

---

1. Although I wasn't initially aware of it, I believe I borrowed the title for this chapter from Art Lindsley, *Love The Ultimate Apologetic: The Heart of Christian Witness* (Downers Grove: InterVarsity Press, 2008). I recommend this work.

of faith, in radical relationship to God, are called to be fla orful salt and a shining light."²

This passage serves to highlight a theme that is all too often neglected in our discussions of Christian apologetics and far too often lacking in our lives. People are attracted to the faith and drawn into a relationship with God when they see God's love expressed. Love demonstrated is more important than an academic forum or an intellectual defense. Of course these are not mutually exclusive, and there is no need to choose one over the other. It is important to recognize, however, that whatever arguments we provide, however sound our intellectual processes, these will remain ineffecti e apart from this "shining" about which Jesus speaks. Love, in other words, is the central apologetic, for it allows everything else that we say or do to find esonance with those whom God calls to Himself.

A sampling of relevant texts will help to make this clear:

• John 13 –

John's Gospel records that Jesus showed His love for others by washing His disciples' feet (John 13:1-17). This, He did as "an example" (15). If the Master, i.e., Jesus, served others, how much more must we? A little later in the same chapter, Jesus utters this challenge:

> A new command I give you: Love one another. As I have loved you, so you must love one another. By this all men will know that you are my disciples, if you love one another (John 13:34-35).

The focus, once again, is love, in this case the love of Jesus' disciples for one another. When this attitude permeates a faith community, it has an impact on outsiders. What Jesus is saying, in other words, is that our sacrificial concern for others, our willingness to love people (both within and outside of the church), is an apologetic that gives expression to the fact that we are His.

---

2. Elaine A. Robinson, *Godbearing: Evangelism Reconceived* (Cleveland, OH: The ilgrim Press, 2006), 98.

▪ John 15 –

The necessity of love is made clear in John 15:17, which reads as follows: "This I command you, that you love one another." Jesus is straightforward and to the point, and this is no mere word of advice. Instead, it takes the form of a command. To care for other believers and–by way of extension–those without faith, is not an option but rather the essence of our created and redemptive purpose. God has sent His Son, and His Son's requirements can be boiled down to this: "Love one another."

Later in John 15, the author addresses the subject of misunderstanding and persecution, which are sure to occur when someone seeks to follow Jesus. Yet, despite difficulties those who follow Him are to retain a love for one another and for all people. Jesus even promises the aid of the Holy Spirit, who testifies of od's Son:

> When the Helper comes, whom I will send to you from the Father, that is the Spirit of truth who proceeds from the Father, He will testify about me, and you will testify also, because you have been with Me from the beginning (John 15:26-27).[3]

Though, in one sense, the world–the organized system that dishonors truth and righteousness–is outside the scope of Jesus' immediate focus, being rather the recipient of divine displeasure, in another sense, some of those within the world will indeed hear the message and believe. For the sake of others, and with the help of God's Spirit, we must demonstrate love.

▪ John 17 –

In this passage, Jesus reflects on the relationship He has with God and how this spills over into the lives of those who follow Him. "I have made Your name known to them, and will make it known so that the love with which You loved Me may be in them, and I in them" (John 17:26).

Again, Jesus prays to His Father, asking that their shared love (i.e., as Father and Son) would fl w into the lives of others. In other

---

3. Though the immediate reference is to the first disciples, the broader application seems to include future followers, as well (Cf. John 17:20).

words the love that originates in the triune God is revealed to us. Experiencing this love in all of its personal, infinite, and emotional intensity, transforms us and enables us, in turn, to share this love, God's love, with others.

▪ Luke 6 –

Luke further explores this motif as he records the command to love our enemies, seeking the betterment of even those who hate, curse, and mistreat us. Jesus expects that we will live in a way that is driven by mercy (Luke 6:32-36). The "golden rule" summarizes this: "Treat others the same way you want them to treat you" (Luke 6:31).

Again, it is plain to see that followers of Jesus are to embody a distinct lifestyle, one in which love is the dominant theme and motivation. If we are to have a positive influence in the lives of others, it will be by means of a sincere concern for their well-being.

▪ Colossians 4 –

Colossians adds to this mix of practical, others-centered injunctions.

> Be wise in the way you act toward outsiders; make the most of every opportunity. Let your conversation be always full of grace, seasoned with salt, so that you may know how to answer everyone (Colossians 4:5-6).

"Outsider" is not a pejorative term but a description of those who do not currently embrace Jesus. These individuals, our fellow human beings, are to be the recipients of our love. Far from being "religious projects," they are people we should appreciate and care for.

When given the opportunity, we must assist others, which includes interacting with them and sharing what we know of the good news. To this end our conversation is to be "full of grace." Contrary to the defensive and critical approaches that abound, our lives are to be governed by grace, that is, controlled by the overarching recognition that God accepts us freely in Jesus. As a result, we are to treat each case individually, providing what each person requires. The "seasoned with salt" metaphor probably entails living in a manner that improves the spiritual quality of those we encounter. We attract people to the faith, in other words, not by forced presentations or overly judgmental statements but by making the lives of others better. Love, once again, is a powerful component of an authentic apologetic.

▪ 1 Peter 3 –

Another example is found in 1 Peter 3:13-17, which is often used as a proof text for apologetics.[4] This passage tells us to "make a defense" (NIV: "give an answer") and "give an account" (NIV: "the reason") for our hope. What is sometimes missed, however, is the larger context. Our answer and reason, our communication of a clear and cogent *apologia*, will be ineffecti e if we fail to share it with "gentleness and respect" (3:15). Whatever else this entails, a Christian apologetic includes far more than intellectual feasibility and consistency. The driving force of a persuasive apologetic is the life that we live. Specificall , it is our willingness to genuinely care about the people we encounter. Even, as in this text, if we are maligned for our faith, we must keep a clear conscience and maintain proper behavior (3:16-17). Again, love must win the day.

Conclusion

This sampling of texts helps orient us to that which is of utmost importance. We are to love one another, acting as conduits of divine love, sharing our hearts and lives with those God brings our way. The e are many, of course, who have acknowledged the need to love, pointing out the hypocrisy of a message devoid of a changed life. But the life of love is no mere addendum to a Christian apologetic. Indeed, love is the very essence and driving force of apologetics, the chief means through which people are drawn to faith and inspired to join the journey with the Savior.

Christian apologetics can and does involve a number of features. Truth must be explained and misconceptions corrected. Theology must be defended and argued for. False ideas must be countered and replaced with authentic ones. And we must allow the sheer force of proven ideas to hold sway in our lives. But, at the end of the

4. For a more detailed account of this passage, see Chapter 1, Hope's Reason.

day, what truly matters is that we come to the realization that there is—How can we describe it?—love in the universe. This love is real, personal, and most profoundly expressed in the incarnation, life, death, and resurrection of God's unique Son, Jesus. Though Him there is reconciliation with God and one another. Because of Him there is purpose and hope. In Him love takes on a tangible form as the eternal deity becomes a human, thereby joining us to our Maker. Though Jesus, God's love flows through us and out to others. Our responsibility, our honor, is to shine forth this love. To the degree that we do, we engage in the ultimate apologetic.

Excursus:
The Love Dynamic

In Scripture we are commanded to love. The object of our love is to be both God and others (Mark 12:30-31), extending even to those who are our enemies (Matthew 5:44).

To love is to express genuine interest in the well-being of another, actually caring enough (whether we feel like it or not) to seek the benefit of others. This is our highest calling, the life we are called to embrace and embody. But, where does this love originate? What is its ultimate source?

Though we witness love in many realms, the ultimate source of love is God. Indeed, John tells us explicitly that "God is love" (1 John 4:16). At God's very core is this dynamic of love. From all eternity, God has loved, which involves the relationships between the various members of the Godhead. As Grenz states:

> The biblical imperative to love is an anticipated outworking of the principle that the ultimate foundation for human relationships resides in the eternal dynamic of the triune God. Thus, humans fulfill their purpose as destined to be the *imago dei* by loving after the manner of the triune God.[1]

The Christian concept of the trinity (or triunity) is no mere abstract theory; the actual interconnectedness within God makes God who and what God is. Jesus alluded to this theme when He spoke of the love that He shared with His Father "before the foundation of the world" (John 17:24). Of course the greatest demonstration of this

---

1. Stanley J. Grenz, *The Social God and the Relational Self: A Trinitarian Theology of the Imago Dei* (Louisville, KY: Westminster John Knox Press, 2001), 320.

love is God's unique Son, whom God sent to rescue the world (John 3:16). 1 John says it this way:

> By this the love of God was manifested in us, that God has sent His only begotten Son into the world so that we might live through Him. In this is love, not that we loved God, but that He loved us and sent His Son to be the propitiation for our sins (1 John 4:9-10).

Love, therefore, begins within the very nature of God, flows out to us in many ways, most notably through Jesus' life, death, and resurrection. Love is a characteristic and an expression of deity.

But the purpose of all this "love talk" is not merely to provide food for thought or material for someone's lecture. Rather, this love is to impact the way we live our lives, being the chief ingredient of and motivation for positive thought and action. In other words we are to be captivated by God's goodness and amazed by His grace. As 1 John states: "We love, because He first loved us" (4:19). And this love is no mere theory, for it must manifest itself in tangible ways: "Let us not love with word or with tongue, but in deed and truth" (1 John 3:18).

We find this same attitude in various places, including the following:

- "Love one another, even as I have loved you" (John 13:34). Jesus is the ultimate pattern, the One we seek to follow.

- "Beloved, if God so loved us, we also ought to love one another" (1 John 4:11). If God's love is so immense that He would be willing to send His Son for foolish rebels, surely we can seek the same type of love for others.

- "For the love of Christ controls us" (2 Corinthians 5:14). The governing disposition of our lives is that which comes to us through an appreciative awareness of Jesus' love.

- "No one has seen God at any time; if we love one another, God abides in us, and His love is perfected in us" (1 John 4:12). God "shows up" in special ways when we love.

- "We have come to know and have believed the love which God has for us. God is love, and the one who abides in love abides in God, and God abides in him" (1 John 4:16) When we love we are drawn to God and connected to Him in very personal ways.

In sum, there is a dynamic of love that originates with God, emerges from God, and is displayed in many places, most notably in Jesus. We enter into this dynamic by contemplating the mercy and grace we have received, spending time with other recipients of divine favor, and by "rubbing shoulders" with the God of love. The bottom line is this: When we become aware of this love, it inevitably penetrates every part of our lives, making it much more likely that we will reciprocate and love as we have been loved.

Inter-Trinitarian Love

Revealed/Displayed

Received/Experienced

Shared/Reflected

"It is not he that has heard a long description of the sweetness of honey that can be said to have the greatest understanding of it, but he that has tasted."

Jonathan Edwards

"O taste and see that the Lord is good."

Psalm 34:8

Chapter Eight

Conclusion

Long ago, Augustine expressed the longing of the human heart. "Our hearts our restless, Lord, until they rest in thee." As one commentator notes, "We try vainly to fill that void ourselves with all manner of earthly things, some good and some bad, but nothing can heal the eternal ache save the Being who placed it there."[1] Apart from God, we are all incomplete and out of synch with our created purpose. Untied to Him, however, we connect with the One who is worthy of trust, who enables us to live with hope, and who both expresses love and empowers us to do the same.

The preceding chapters (and appendices to follow) are intended to generate thought and discussion about the broad subject of apologetics and how we can best promote and encourage this connection with God. As we have said, a number of factors contribute to this task, some of which have been delineated here. Among other things, our apologetic must fl w out of the biblical witness, locating its emphases and priorities in divine revelation. Likewise, from a theological point of view, it will be important to rightly perceive what human beings, the real-life recipients of the gospel, are truly like, for only then will we be able to actually interact with them in meaningful ways. This includes an awareness of our social milieu, a recognition that we are in the midst of widespread cultural change,

---

1. Louis Markos, *Lewis Agonistes: How C. S. Lewis Can Train Us to Wrestle with the Modern and Postmodern World* (Nashville, TN: Broadman & Holman Publishers, 2003), 42.

and a realization that we need much discernment if we are going to distinguish between harmful and (potentially) helpful trends.

In many ways, our *apologia* must seek a kind of spiritual poise, balancing commitment and adaptive abilities (some things change and others do not), confidence and humility (speaking with a measure of certainty but always remaining open to change), intellectual facts and emotional appeals (thinking and feeling are both essential), arguments for the truth and a lifestyle that embodies the truth (our words and lives work together). Indeed, these and other components must be held in tension as we ourselves journey with God, seeking ways to improve our witness for the gospel.

From the realm of academia to the domain of the lunch room, from the classroom to the water cooler, from the deeply philosophical to the down-to-earth, from the coffee shop to the bar stool, during good times and bad, our great honor and joy is to guide others to the One who is "the way, and the truth, and the life" (John 14:6). This, in part, is what it means to "give an account for the hope that is in you" (1 Peter 3:15).

"Make sure that when you leave a person, he is closer to Jesus than when you first met him."

Anonymous

Appendix A

Conversion and Apologetic Expectations

If the goal of apologetics is to make a clear and compelling case for the believability and appeal of the Christian gospel, it is important to ask ourselves what we're actually looking for. If we are going to assist people in seeking the truth, we must be clear about what the truth is and what it looks like in the real world. Broadly speaking, what does it mean to follow Jesus?

To follow Jesus is to acknowledge His Lordship and embrace Him as Savior. Once the eternal God became human, He lived in this world, died in our place, and conquered death on our behalf. In Him there is rescue, restoration, hope, and power to live a God-honoring life. According to Scripture, we receive these benefits and are united to Him by faith.

Faith, then, is the way to God. This faith is not some vague notion that everything will eventually work out (though we believe it will). It is not reliance upon humanity's goodness or our personal virtues. For that matter, it's not believing in whatever strikes one's fancy. Rather, faith, if it is true, is trust in the one known as Jesus of Nazareth. As apologists, our goal is to direct others to Him, which of course necessitates that we distinguish between true and false objects of faith, between Jesus and anything or anyone else.

But genuine faith ushers in a changed life. As John puts it, we "walk in the light" (1 John 1:7), "keep His commandments" (1 John 2:4), confess that "Jesus Christ has come in the fles " (4:2), and, among other things, "love one another" (4:11). In other words there are reasonably clear indicators that a person has crossed over from darkness to light (Ephesians 5:8; 1 Thessalonians 5:5)

It is at this point, however, that matters become somewhat unclear. First of all, we cannot actually peer into the hearts of people; that ability belongs to God alone. Nor can we be certain if a person is within God's saving grasp; only God can determine such things.[1]

What complicates matters further is the fact that faith does not look the same in all people. Though there are general characteristics of salvific faith (e.g., holiness, love) and while certain behaviors are obviously prohibited (e.g., lying, adultery), there is disagreement about many things. What are the rules for dating? Is it permissible to attend an R-Rated movie? What type of clothing is appropriate? How often should one attend church? What kind of relationship is a believer to have with secular society? Probably more than most of us realize, we assume a variety of things about others, things that we deem part and parcel of the Christian experience. If you are a believer in Jesus, you will act a certain way, do certain things, and utter certain familiar verbiage.

The problem, however, is that it is all too easy to confuse personal or ecclesiastical traditions with the truth of Scripture. Indeed, one of the weaknesses of many apologetic encounters is the tendency to mistake the assumptions of our particular Christian subculture with what God has said. When this occurs–and I think it's common–it not only confuses and frustrates our hearers but actually serves to diminish the power of our message. God has promised that His Word will not return without fulfilling His intentions (Isaiah 55:11). This means that big issues of truth and love will win the day, for they are "backed" by God's promise and presence. But, when we assume as apologists (and as Christians in general) that *our* cultural, societal, and personal pathways to God are the only ones, we actually assume too much. God has not put His imprimatur on the grids we have created but on His Word. To the degree that we conflate the two, e hinder the work of apologetics.

The presumptuous attitude that others must mirror our particular practices is all to familiar. It is, perhaps, most obvious among

---

1. This is not to deny that we can indeed make reasonable judgments based on the fruit or lack thereof in a person's life (Matthew 7:17). It's just that we are ill equipped to make any final judgments, for only God can see into the human heart (1 Samuel 16:7).

missionaries to foreign lands, who have sometimes been guilty of confusing traditional religious practices (the way we dress or conduct worship) with the gospel itself (the truth that Jesus rescues and restores). But it is also something found in Western evangelistic endeavors. In other words it is inappropriate for us to expect everyone to follow our dress code (suit coats on Sunday, a certain length dress), use our lingo ("Praise the Lord"), and follow precisely defined behavior (Don't drink, curse, or smoke!).

As we interact with others and hope for their conversion, our task can become amazingly complex. This complexity is a result of our tendency to make judgments too quickly, applying personal agendas that become easily entangled with the good news itself. What God is doing in a person's life (or the pace at which He's doing it) may not match our own assumptions.

But the gospel itself provides a simpler way ahead, for the biblical message involves free access to God through His Son. Our privilege is to share this message with others, trusting *Him* with the results. In the final analysis, therefore, we must recognize and be satisfied with the fact that salvation is God's business and not something we orchestrate. Our duty is to be faithful, telling others of Jesus and, at least as important, expressing His love to others.

It is, therefore, necessary to acknowledge, within the parameters of Scripture, that we cannot assume that conversion will produce men and women who look and act exactly like we do. True faith will manifest itself in ways that vary from person to person and situation to situation. As we look with excitement for the fruit of our apologetic labors, our expectations must be shaped by Scripture (not our treasured opinions) and governed by humility (not our personal comfort levels).[2]

---

2. Though it is beyond the scope of our treatment here, many other issues arise when considering the topic of human salvation. How much knowledge must a person possess in order to be converted? How much ignorance or error can be present in the life of a genuinely converted individual? And what about those who never hear the gospel? These and related questions have stirred debate for centuries. For a fascinating look at these subjects, see Terrance L. Tiessen, *Who Can Be Saved? Reassessing Salvation in Christ* (Downers Grove. IL InterVarsity Press, 2004). Tiessen approaches these matters from an orthodox Christian perspective, seeking to make sense of all of the biblical data. Whether or not one agrees with his conclusions, he certainly fosters a helpful discussion about our part and God's in the process of evangelism and conversion.

Appendix B

Brief Lessons from Jesus on Relating to the World

If we are going to be faithful in our relationships with others, it helps to have examples to follow, and none is better than Jesus. What follows are a number of brief observations about Jesus and how He related to others.

1. **Jesus spent time with regular people, focusing especially on the downtrodden and those who were going through hard times.**

    The e was no arrogance or party spirit with Jesus. He was never an elitist. How often are we?

2. **Jesus wasn't afraid to break with tradition.**

    What a paradigm breaker He was! Of course what makes His "break with tradition" especially striking and surprising to many is the fact that he often separated himself from religiously-minded people. The e are times, perhaps, when we will have to do the same.

3. **Jesus' chief opposition came from the orthodox defenders of his day, those (supposedly) already within the fold of the faithful.**

    This is a remarkable lesson to learn. If we fail to pay attention, we place ourselves in a rather precarious position. The Pharisees of Jesus' day gave every appearance of being the "real deal." That is, they were not–as typically imagined–so obvious in their hypocrisy. Had we lived in their day, we would no doubt have applauded many of their commitments and traditions. Yet, at least in some cases, they were hypocritical. How often, I wonder, are we?

4. **Jesus primary targets of attack were these same religious hypocrites.**

   This is another strange but true fact about the Savior of the world. He spent more time criticizing and correcting the people who were the best informed than He did those who were clearly, in most people's eyes, outside of the faith community. Scarey thoughts indeed.

5. **Jesus rarely felt hurried or pressured in his relationships with others.**

   Though there might have been a couple of well-chosen exceptions, Jesus' general strategy was to spend whatever time He could with people, and He never seemed to be in a rush or prone to use pressure tactics. While He cared deeply about the spiritual condition of those He encountered, His strategy for assisting them was not forced or overly predictable. Do we possess the faith and patience to follow His example?

6. **Jesus specialized in story telling.**

   He didn't feel like He had to frame everything according to logical categories or present the truth in neat little packages. Rather, He utilized stories to provide a more personal look into what God had done, was doing, and would do. Narrative drew people into a relationship with truth that included but was never limited to abstract ideas. When was the last time you told a good (God-honoring) story?

7. **Jesus was the epitome of compassion and love.**

   He was driven by compassion and a desire to help people, many of whom were blinded to the truth and resistant to the idea of following the Spirit into a relationship with God. Jesus' life and ministry, His choices and decisions, were all governed by a zeal for his Father's kingdom and for the hearts and lives of those He met. Are we at all like Him?

8. **Jesus went to where the people were, unhindered by religiously defined parameters of acceptable behavior.**

   The e was no "sacred vs. secular" with the Son of God. Just about everything was (potentially, at least) sacred. Indeed, it might be argued that the locations that were supposed to be the meeting places of God (temple, synagogue) were often the very places where He was least likely to be found. Have we limited the activity of God to the so-called religious realm? Do we look for God in the everyday occurrences of life?

9. **Jesus wasn't afraid to speak the truth, whether to friend or foe.**

   Jesus was clearly a person of great courage. He had the courage to leave his Father's side in order to reside among human beings. He was bold enough to stand against evil, even when that evil resided in the religious establishment. He had the guts to endure the incomprehensible agony of being judged by God for wrongs *we* had committed. Lord, give us grace and courage, as well.

10. **Jesus often used an indirect approach in His efforts to reach others.**

    That is, Jesus rarely said the things we presume He did, things like "believe in Me," "ask Me to come into your heart," etc. Sometimes, of course, He did say things like this, but more times than not He spent time with people, told them stories, and gently though powerfully invited them into the realm of divine love and acceptance, that is, into the presence of God. He wasn't trying to press for a "decision," for apparently that's not the way relationships are established and hearts molded.

    Though this subject surely deserves much more treatment, it is plain to see that Jesus, the perfect paradigm of spiritual assistance, is our greatest example. Are we paying attention? In seeking to share the truth with others, are we filling to follow Him?

Appendix C

The Templates Through Which We See the World

We all look at the world a certain way. Whether we've actually analyzed it or not, we see life through the "glasses" that are a part of who and what we currently are. In other words we all approach life–from parenting to philosophy, from education to relationships–with presuppositions. These presuppositions serve as a template of sorts, an interpretive grid through which we perceive just about everything.

That being the case, it is important that we presuppose properly. While I have no full-proof formula, and though I am as prone to error as anyone, a number of ideas come to mind, including the following:

- **Be aware that you have presuppositions.**

It's amazing how two people can look at the same information, the same facts, and interpret them diffe ently. One person interprets an argument as a purely negative event, while another sees it as an opportunity to clear the air and make things right. One person views strong competition as that which breeds failure and lowers self-esteem, while another views the same level of competition as an opportunity to improve. Of course we all tend to be fickle about a good many things, and so it's not always easy to discern what our assumptions are. The point, though, is that we always assume something whenever we interpret reality. Our eyes are just that, *ours*. The "lenses" through which we see the world are *our* lenses.

One immensely helpful idea, therefore, is to simply realize that we all assume various things when we look at life. Realizing this fact frees us from having to prove everything, for not everything can be demonstrated, at least not easily. Furthermore, it enables us to recognize that we, like everyone else, make assumptions along the way. If these prove valid, we can retain them. If, on the other hand, we recognize some flaw in our own assumptions, we can tweak or even reject our current viewpoint. None of this can happen, however, unless we at least realize that–for better or worse–we presuppose many things.

- **Some presuppositions are better than others.**

How, though, do we determine whose presuppositions are right and whose are invalid? Sometimes, we can simply look at the facts and, to the best of our ability, determine that certain things are correct and others incorrect. A part of this relates to our historical context and the experiences we've had. If someone says that 2 + 2 = 5, we can show that such a view runs contrary to human experience with numbers and contradicts certain points of logic. In some areas, though, it will be difficul to prove with absolute certainty that "this" is a better option than "that." At times, it is probably helpful, at least with certain individuals, to point out the usefulness of a given option. Certain ideas (e.g., liberty, freedom, fairness) have a history of success that is superior to other ideas (e.g., slavery, injustice). Not all will be convinced, of course, but some will, which is a good thing.

Depending on the issue at hand, the validity of certain views (e.g., certain areas of science) might be shown through research and by sifting through the current data. But, at the end of the day, I think we need to truly embrace the idea that there is a type of reason, sensibleness, and logic, a kind of correctness, embedded into the universe. Thus, in the long run, the truth will eventually surface because there is a truth-maker. This, too, is a presupposition, and, I think, a helpful one.

Appendix C

- **Life is designed to be a faith venture.**

This relates to the previous point. It seems that all of life demands faith. If we make claims of logic, we automatically assume such things as the reality of the universe and the reliability of our cognitive equipment. If we make a moral judgment, we assume a moral code and, possibly, a morality making deity. Faith, then, is embedded into the fabric of our lives. Though we can, of course, demonstrate many things, we are never afforded a faith-free access to the world. Whether or not our faith is in the right object, faith itself, even if it's faith that there is no God, is inevitable. Of course believing that the moon is made of green cheese is not as convincing to most as, say, the effects of gravity. In any case, however, there is indeed the need for faith.

If this is the way the world has been constructed, one wonders whether this faith principle has been placed here on purpose. On a Christian reading of history, the necessity of faith is a reminder that the living God yearns for our attention, calling us to trust in and follow him.

If this faith venture is something that is woven into the fabric of the world we inhabit, there might be a corresponding reality to this impulse. While we obviously cannot create gods out of whole cloth, it could be that the true God, the God who placed this faith principle within each of us, is actually "out there" to respond to our acts of faith, hear our prayers, and interact with those who call on His name. Indeed, this is the Christian response to life, looking to the true God, the only God there is, and allowing our lives to connect with His.

- **We can know some things, but perfect or complete knowledge will always evade us.**

Truth is available. At least on a Christian understanding, there is true stuff in the world, stuff we can access. Whatever our official views on many things, we all assume this principle each day. Though we may call ourselves relativists or agnostics, we all intuitively react to life as if it contains elements of truth, things on which we basically "hang our hats."

That said, it is also painfully clear that we have nothing close to prefect or complete knowledge. Much evades our grasp and probably always will. And even the things we know with a measure of confidence a e known in part.

Only God possesses complete knowledge, and this, I think, tells us something about what we should presuppose (from a Christian angle) about ourselves. If we are created in God's image, the image of a knowing deity, it makes sense that *we* would be able to know, as well. On the other hand, given that we are creatures (and not the Creator), it also makes sense that there would be severe limitations in all of our effo ts to know.

The way ahead, therefore, seems to involve the intersection of these two ideas. We can know, which is what makes knowledge a legitimate (indeed, necessary) venture. But we can never know fully, which ought to make us humble, propelling us forward in our quest to better know, and compelling us to look outside of ourselves to the One who alone can guide our effo ts.

Okay, enough said for now. My point, simply, is that we all place our various templates on the world as we attempt to make sense of it. This, in my view, is not a bad thing, however, for it forces us to acknowledge our need of God; this, I would argue, is ultimately for our good. After all, isn't He the One who said that He honors the humble in heart? I suppose–here comes another presupposition–that our job, therefore, is to presuppose humbly yet confidentl , knowing that as we walk by faith we do not walk alone.

Appendix D

WFD in a PM World[1]

Christians have long recognized that there is opposition in this life to the ways of God, hindrances to the walk of faith. Typically, these have been delineated as the World, the Flesh, and the Devil (WFD).

"The world" is a term used by Jesus and the biblical writers to describe the prevalent anti-God atmosphere that permeates human society (John 15:18-19; 1 Corinthians 2:12; 1 John 5:4). The trends that mislead, the attitudes that run contrary to divine wisdom, the choices that fly in the face of God's will, these are said to be of "the world."

Next, there is "the flesh" which refers to the inner human inclinations to violate God's commands, the tendency within us all to ignore our created purpose. Everything that is wrong about us is related to our fallen nature and character. This is why Peter, for example, can write of those who "indulge the flesh in its corrupt desires" (2 Peter 2:10).

Finally, there is the devil, who, according to Scripture, is a personal being of rebellion, the ally and instigator of evil. Whatever one's view of the paranormal, the Bible clearly teaches that nefarious forces, living unseen entities, vie for our attention and seek to lead us astray. In fact the world is said to "lie in the power of the evil one" (1 John 5:19).

---

1. The following is reproduced from the e-zine Next-Wave, which explores issues of church and culture. See http://www.the-next-wave.org.

The World, the Flesh, and Devil. We need not enter into detailed discussion of this three-pronged attack on spiritual well-being. It is enough to acknowledge that people make bad choices, wrong philosophies allure the unsuspecting, deception is an inescapable reality within any age, even a postmodern one.

The purpose here is simply to remind those of us who seek to postmodernize the faith, who desire to be on the cutting edge of what God is doing in our day, that we are not immune to falsehood. Indeed, it is often the case that harmful influences show up at precisely the time when God is most active. We should be aware, therefore, that ungodliness can show up during a revival, and pride is never far from even the humblest servant. But, what about now? Where might the demonic appear today? In what ways is the emerging church particularly prone to the temptations of the WFD?

Of course, from the perspective of the emerging church, it is precisely the traditionalists who went astray, having been duped by the WFD (though they might not state it exactly this way). Having succumbed to some of the more questionable presuppositions of the enlightenment, modern Christianity confused cultural ideals with biblical ones. Indeed, the emergence of an alternative (postmodern) view is due, in great part, to an increased perception of (and frustration over) these faulty ways. Postmoderns, in other words, are of the opinion that the traditional church has, on many points, been misled.

But how ironic it would be if, in criticizing others, we failed to see our own shortcomings. For this reason, it is all the more important for postmoderns to be cognizant of their own negative tendencies. What follows is a short list of ways in which the emerging church opens itself up to imbalance and, worse, deception.

- When modern hubris is (rightly) condemned but is done so in a condescending way, something is amiss. Pride is something that no age can completely avoid.

- Similarly, when dogmatism is opposed dogmatically, we are clearly off target. Sometimes, as mentioned above, this is evidence that we postmoderns cannot escape our worst qualities. Other times, it simply demonstrates that a certain kind of dogmatism still has a place in the emerging church.

Appendix D

- Likewise, when postmodern humility (a potentially wonderful commodity) starts to sound like naivete, it's time to reevaluate. We need more caution and discernment, but foolishness and an unwillingness to stand for the ways of God are never good.
- When reason is minimized through the use of reasoned argumentation, perhaps we have "thrown out the baby with the bath water." Reason as the sole arbiter of truth is a modern myth, but reason as one facet of the image of God is an unavoidable (and potentially healthy) thing.
- When the significance of narrative is stated in propositional form ("Thou shalt preach the narrative portions of Scripture"), one wonders how postmoderns miss the fact that, as meaningful as the stories of Scripture are, propositions deserve more than lip service (after all, "Jesus is Lord" is a proposition). Stories must be returned to their proper place in the life of the church, but propositions (especially when tied to these stories!) mustn't be forgotten.
- When community (a much needed emphasis) becomes so nebulous that it actually interferes with the needs of the individual, it might be time to take a closer look at what we are promoting. While there is something special and refreshing about community, the noble effo ts to embody this corporate concept must never interfere with personal accountability and the life of each individual believer.
- When the quest for an experiential faith doesn't recognize that experience should be fostered through truth ("sound doctrine" – e.g., 1 Timothy 4:6; 6:3), perhaps we have failed to provide the proper (biblically oriented) contexts for these experiences.
- When the written word is treated as passe *through the medium of print*, one wonders if some postmoderns even notice the inconsistency. The emerging chu ch can still learn via books.
- When image is emphasized with hardly a thought about the possibility of idolatry (visible or conceptual), it may be time to sit up and take notice.

Please don't misunderstand. The purpose of these illustrations is not to "throw a wet blanket" on the postmodern motifs mentioned above, and I am certainly *not* advocating a "three steps forward, two steps back" approach. Indeed, it is my contention that we must consciously highlight such notions as community, mystery, humility, experience, and creativity. May God keep us from getting in the way of the wonderful things He is doing in this postmodern era.

At the same time, it is good to occasionally pause and look at ourselves. In our quest to catch the wave of God's new dealings, amid the rejuvenated feeling of being in on something that is truly grand and wonderful, let us never think that we have arrived. Though God is providing a renewal of church, our hearts are still deceitful. While the Lord of history is actively leading us to embrace certain cultural trends, the world is still a dangerous place. Though our hearts resonate with Spirit-driven topics, the heart can still be a factory of idols, the inner chamber where half-truths sap the very life out of us.

WFD–the World, the Flesh, and the Devil–they still compete for our attention, seeking to take God's people captive through the misuse of opportunities, and by means of the simplistic belief that these nemeses have little impact in today's world. May the Lord preserve us from error, and may we learn to journey together through this world, excited by what God is doing but also cognizant that, in the end, what will matter most is not our ability to postmodernize the faith but that we faithfully serve the Rock of (all) ages, postmodern and beyond.

Bibliography

Anderson, Ray S. *The Shape of Practical Theology: Empowering Ministry with Theological Praxis*. Downers Grove, IL: InterVarsity Press, 2001.

———. *An Emergent Theology for Emerging Churches*. Downers Grove, IL: InterVarsity Press, 2006.

Barna, George. *The Second Coming of the Church*. Nashville, TN: Word Publishing, 1998.

Barnes, Albert. *Barnes' Notes on the New Testament*. Grand Rapids, MI: Kregel Publishers, 1976.

Boa, Kenneth and Robert M. Bowman Jr. *Faith Has Its Reasons: An Integrative Approach to Defending Christianity*. Colorado Springs, CO: Navpress Publishing Group, 2001

Bruce, F. F. *The Book of Acts*, New International Commentary on the New Testament. Grand Rapids, MI: William B. Eerdmans Publishing Company, 1988.

———. *The Acts of the Apostles: The Greek Text with Introduction and Commentary*. Grand Rapids, MI: William B. Eerdmans Publishing Company, 1990.

Campbell-Jack, Campbell and Gavin J. McGrath. Eds. *New Dictionary of Christian Apologetics*. Downers Grove, IL: InterVarsity Press, 2006.

Carson, D. A. *The Gagging of God: Christianity Confronts Pluralism*. Grand Rapids, MI: Zondervan Publishing House, 1996.

———. "Athens Revisited" in *Telling the Truth: Evangelizing Postmoderns*, ed. D. A. Carson. Grand Rapids, MI: Zondervan Publishing House, 2000.

Clark, Kelly James. *When Faith Is Not Enough*. Grand Rapids, MI: William B. Eerdmans Publishing Company, 1997.

Comfort, P. W. "Idolatry" in *The Dictionary of Paul and His Letters*. Downers Grove, IL: InterVarsity Press, 1993.

Cowan, Steven B. ed., *Five Views of Apologetics*, The Counterpoint Series. Grand Rapids, MI: Zondervan Publishing House, 2000.

Curtis, Brent and John Eldredge. *The Sacred Romance: Drawing Closer to the Heart of God*. Nashville, TN: Thomas elson Publisher, 1997.

Daryl, Charles J. "Engaging the (Neo) Pagan Mind: Paul's Encounter with Athenian Culture as a Model for Cultural Apologetics (Acts 17:16-34)" in *The Gospel and Contemporary Perspectives: Viewpoints from the Trinity Journal*, ed. Douglas Moo. Grand Rapids, MI: Kregel Publications, 1997.

DiCello, Carmen C. *Dangerous Blessing: The Emergence of a Postmodern Faith*. Eugene, OR: Wipf & Stock Publishers, 2005.

_____. *Why? Reflections on the Problem of Evil*. Eugene, OR: Wipf & Stock Publishers, 2007.

Dodd, Patton. *My Faith So Far : A Story of Conversion and Confusion*. San Francisco, CA: Jossey-Bass, 2005.

Dulles, Avery Cardinal. *A History of Apologetics*. San Francisco, CA: Ignatius Press, 1999.

Erickson, Millard J. *Concise Dictionary of Christian Theology*. Grand Rapids, MI: Baker Book House, 1986.

Evans, C. Stephen. *Why Believe?: Reason and Mystery as Pointers to God*. Grand Rapids, MI: William B. Eerdmans Publishing Company, 1996.

Feinberg, Paul D. "Epistemology" in *Evangelical Dictionary of Theology*, Ed. Walter A. Elwell. Grand Rapids, MI: Baker Book House, 1984.

Fernando, Ajith. *Acts*, The NIV Application Commentary. Grand Rapids, MI: Zondervan Publishing House, 1998.

Frame, John M. *The Doctrine of the Knowledge of God*. Phillipsburg, NJ: Presbyterian and Reformed Publishing Company, 1987.

_____. *Apologetics to the Glory of God*. Phillipsburg, NJ: Presbyterian and Reformed Publishing Company, 1994.

_____. *Cornelius Van Til: An Analysis of His Thought*. Phillipsburg, NJ: Presbyterian and Reformed Publishing Company, 1995.

Goppelt, Leonhard. *A Commentary on I Peter*. Grand Rapids, MI: William B. Eerdmans Publishing Company, 1993.

Green, Michael and Alister McGrath. *How Shall We Reach Them? Defending and Communicating the Christian Faith to Nonbelievers*. Nashville, TN: Thomas Nelson Publishers, 1995.

Grenz, Stanley J. *A Primer on Postmodernism*. Grand Rapids, MI: William B. Eerdmans Publishing Company, 1996.

_____. *The Social God and the Relational Self: A Trinitarian Theology of the Imago Dei*. Louisville, KY: Westminster John Knox Press, 2001.

Grenz, Stanley J., David Guretzki, and Cherith Fee Nordling, "Immanence" in *Pocket Dictionary of Theological Terms*. Downers Grove, IL: InterVarsity Press, 1999.

Helm, Paul. "Faith, Evidence, and the Scriptures" in *Scripture and Truth*, Eds. D. A. Carson and John D. Woodbridge. Grand Rapids, MI: Baker Books, 1992.

Hemer, Colin J. *The Book of Acts in the Setting of Hellenistic History*. Winona Lake, IN: Eisenbrauns, 1990.

Hovestol, Tom. *Extreme Righteousness: Seeing Ourselves in the Pharisees*. Chicago, IL: Moody Press, 1997.

Kimball, Dan. *The Emerging Church: Vintage Christianity for New Generations*. Grand Rapids, MI: Zondervan Publishing House, 2003.

Bibliography

Knight, Henry H. *A Future for Truth: Evangelical Theology in a Postmodern World*. Nashville, TN: Abington Press, 1997.

Kreeft, Peter. *Christianity for Modern Pagans: Pascal's Pensées Edited, Outlined, and Explained*. San Francisco, CA: Ignatius Press, 1993.

Larkin, William J. Jr. *Acts*. Downers Grove, IL: InterVarsity Press, 1995.

Leithart, Peter J. *Solomon Among the Postmoderns*. Grand Rapids, MI: Brazos Press, 2008.

Lewis, C. S. *The Weight of Glory*. New York: HarperCollins Publishers, 2001.

Lindsley, Art. *Love The Ultimate Apologetic: The Heart of Christian Witness*. Downers Grove, IL: InterVarsity Press, 2008.

Long, Jimmy. *Generating Hope: A Strategy for Reaching the Postmodern Generation*. Downers Grove, IL: InterVarsity Press, 1997.

Markos, Louis. *Lewis Agonistes: How C. S. Lewis Can Train Us to Wrestle with the Modern and Postmodern World*. Nashville, TN: Broadman & Holman Publishers, 2003.

Marshall, I. H. *Acts*. Grand Rapids, MI: William B. Eerdmans Publishing Company, 1980.

_____. *1 Peter*, The IVP New Testament Series. Downers Grove, IL: InterVarsity Press, 1991.

Mayers, Ronald B. *Balanced Apologetics: Using Evidence and Presuppositions in Defense of the Faith*. Grand Rapids, MI: Kregel Publications, 1984.

McKnight, Scot. *1 Peter*, The NIV Application Commentary. Grand Rapids, MI: Zondervan Publishing House, 1996.

McLaren, Brian D. *A Generous Orthodoxy*. Grand Rapids, MI: Zondervan Publishing House, 2004.

Michaels, J. Ramsey. *1 Peter*, Word Biblical Commentary, Vol 49. Waco, TX.: Word Books, 1988.

Miller, Donald. *Blue Like Jazz: Nonreligious Thoughts on Christian Spirituality*. Nashville, TN: Thomas elson Publishers, 2003.

Newbigin, Leslie. *Proper Confidence: Faith, Doubt and Certainty in Christian Discipleship*. Grand Rapids, MI: William B. Eerdmans Publishing Company, 1995.

Otto, Rudolf. *The Idea of the Holy*. New York: Oxford University Press, 1958.

Packer, J. I. *Fundamentalism and the Word of God*. Grand Rapids, MI: William B. Eerdmans Publishing Company, 1988.

Pascal, Blaise. *Pensées*. New York: E. P. Dutton & Co., Inc., 1958.

Prior, Kenneth. *The Gospel in Pagan Society*. Fearn, Ross-shire, Scotland: Christian Focus Publications, 1995.

Robinson, Elaine A. *Godbearing: Evangelism Reconceived*. Cleveland, OH: The Pilgrim Press, 2006.

Sire, James W. *The Universe Next Door: A Basic World View Catalog*. Downers Grove, IL: InterVarsity Press, 1988.

Smith, Chuck Jr. *The End of the World . . . As We Know It*. Colorado Springs, CO: Waterbrook Press, 2001.

Stackhouse, John G. Jr. *Humble Apologetics: Defending the Faith Today*. New York: Oxford University Press, 2002.

Staub, Dick. *Too Christian, Too Pagan*. Grand Rapids, MI: Zondervan Publishing House, 2000.

Stott, John R. W. *The Message of Acts*. Downers Grove, IL: InterVarsity Press, 1990.

Sweet, Leonard I. *Quantum Spirituality: A Postmodern Apologetic*. Dayton, OH: United Theological eminary, 1991.

_____. *Post-Modern Pilgrims: First Century Passion for the 21ˢᵗ Century World*. Nashville, TN: Broadman & Holman Publishers, 2000.

_____. *Carpe Mañana: Is Your Church Ready to Seize Tomorrow?* Grand Rapids, MI: Zondervan Publishing House, 2001.

_____. *The Gospel According to Starbucks: Living With a Grande Passion*. Colorado Springs, CO: Waterbrook Press, 2007.

Tickle, Phyllis. *The Great Emergence: How Christianity is Changing and Why*. Grand Rapids, MI: Baker Books, 2008.

Tiessen, Terrance L. *Who Can Be Saved? Reassessing Salvation in Christ*. Downers Grove. IL InterVarsity Press, 2004.

Williams, David J. *Acts*. Peabody, MA: Hendrickson Publishers, 1990.

Wood, Jay W. *Epistemology: Becoming Intellectually Virtuous*. Downers Grove, IL: InterVarsity Press, 1998.

Wright, N. T. *Simply Christian: Why Christianity Makes Sense*. New York: Harper-Collins Publishers, 2006.

Zacharias, Ravi. *Deliver Us From Evil: Restoring the Soul in a Disintegrating Culture*. Nashville, TN: Word Publishing, 1997.

If you would like to contact Carmen DiCello, he can be reached at carmen1978@comcast.net.

www.ingramcontent.com/pod-product-compliance
Lightning Source LLC
Chambersburg PA
CBHW051105160426
43193CB00010B/1317